VILLAGES
OF
NORTHERN ARGYLL

VILLAGES OF NORTHERN ARGYLL

MARY WITHALL

JOHN DONALD PUBLISHERS
EDINBURGH

First published in 2004 by John Donald Publishers
An imprint of Birlinn Ltd
West Newington House
10 Newington Road
Edinburgh
EH9 1QS

www.birlinn.co.uk

ISBN 0 85976 584 9

British Library Cataloguing-in-Publication Data
A catalogue record for this book is available
from the British Library

Typeset by Brinnoven, Livingston
Printed and bound by Antony Rowe Ltd, Chippenham

CONTENTS

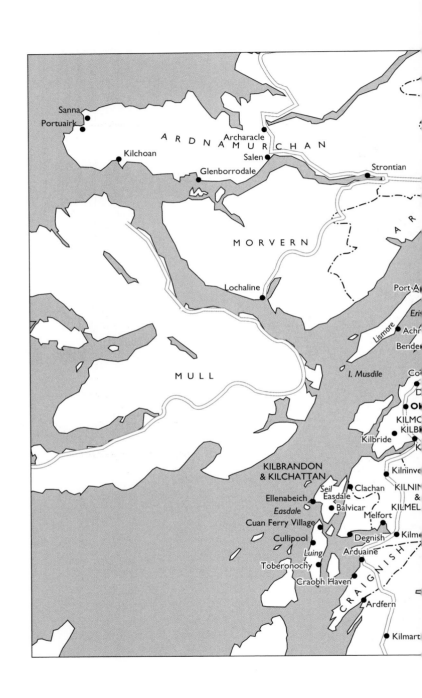

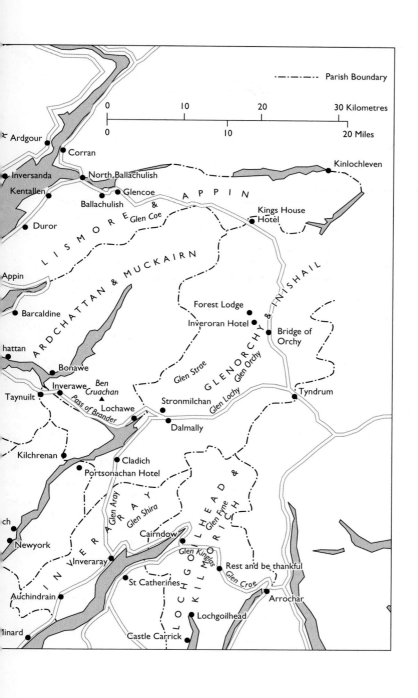

INTRODUCTION

The first-time visitor to the county of Argyll might well be excused for asking the question, 'Villages, what villages?'

There you are driving along the A819 or the A85, admiring the scenery and wondering when you are going to come across a hotel or a tearoom, when a place name suddenly flashes out at you from the side of the road. Scarcely do you have time to reduce speed in a restricted zone before you have passed that black slash on a white background and are accelerating away again into the wild unknown. There has been no time to take in the buildings, facilities, anything. You have just by-passed a village.

Road improvements in the second half of the twentieth century ensured that most settlements in this county of mountains, valleys, sea lochs and fast-flowing rivers, have been bypassed. They can be found, but only by those sufficiently inquisitive to turn off the main road and take one of the narrow country roads which once represented the only routes through the Highlands. Even then the small collection of buildings – a church, a row of cottages, a pub, perhaps even a nineteenth-century villa or two – gives little clue as to what went on here in the past or what it was that persuaded people to set up home in such an obscure and lonely place.

In order to understand how the Argyll villages came to be sited where they are, we have to take a closer look at the people of past centuries who managed to make their mark upon a landscape which offers so little opportunity for change.

Towards the end of the last Ice Age, when sea levels were low, Great Britain was still joined in part to the Continent of Europe. The earliest settlers walked in, we believe, from northern Europe, following in the path of wandering herds of game animals. Their long journey ended at last when they reached the Atlantic seaboard of Argyll and gazed outwards beyond the islands to the wide Atlantic Ocean.

Neolithic Man, seeking protection from evil spirits, wild animals and marauding tribesmen, chose to dwell in caves or in strongholds which were surrounded by water. Argyll provided ample opportunity for both kinds of settlement and throughout the region there is

Cairn above Kintraw (*Author's Collection*)

evidence of human habitation dating back to more than five thousand years before Christ and the coming of Christian missionaries. Cave dwellings and crannogs or man-made islands, built on the shallow margins of many of the lochs, earthworks and brochs, show us where and how early Man lived, while the cairns and cists in which they buried their dead provide evidence of their belief in gods and in an after-life. More importantly, perhaps, these relics provide clues as to why they chose to settle in one place rather than another.

In seeking suitable places to live early Man looked for shelter from the weather, an abundance of food, protection from attack and adequate supplies of water and fuel. When manufacture and trading began, local supplies of raw materials became equally important in choosing a place to settle. The discovery of metals such as iron, lead and copper led to the manufacture of weapons, tools for agriculture and goods for barter. Coal provided fuel for cooking and heating. The oak woods provided bark for the tanning of leather and lichens for dyeing cloth. Birch woods could be coppiced for the manufacture of charcoal for fuel. As agriculture began to take the place of hunting and gathering food, people moved from the safety of the high ground and their islands in the loch, to the more fertile loch shores and river valleys where they could grow grain and root crops and where animals might be raised on lush pastures. Still wary of their neighbours, however, they built earthworks, brochs or forts. These were large

Standing stone above Kintraw, overlooking Loch Creignish (*Author's Collection*)

enough, should they be attacked, for everyone to retreat inside with their stocks of grain and all their animals.

Individual tribes, or clans, huddled together in their isolation eking out an existence from the surrounding countryside. They resisted all attempts at infiltration by others, and were warlike, aggressive and avaricious, often raiding the settlements of their neighbours for cattle, crops or women. It was in this strange environment, so closely dependent upon the forces of Nature, that the Celtic traditions flourished. Natural phenomena such as the elements were deified. Wild beasts, the mountains that enclosed their world, the streams and trees were given human characters. Despite the isolation of the separate tribes, ideas appear to have developed universally for, no matter how a body of people might try to prevent it, new blood was

Comcuille – 1997 – re-enactment of the voyage of St Columba (*Author's Collection*)

bound to come in whether in the form of captives, waifs and strays or as the result of marriages between tribes.

It was to this world, ruled by the spirits of the water and the beasts of the forests and mountains that missionaries from Ireland came in the sixth century AD. They called the area Earra Ghaidheal (Argyll: coastland of the Gael) in the language of the Irish priests. Arriving by sea they settled at the margins of the country. In celebration of the 1,400th anniversary of St Columba's death, in 1997 a group of pilgrims from Ireland re-enacted the priest's voyage in a replica currach of timber, canvas and tar, rowing and sailing their vessel to Iona and other sites along the coast of Argyll. The vessel, 11.2 m in length and 2.4 m wide, was powered only by a set of lug sails, twelve oarsmen and a navigator.

It was to be many centuries before there was significant settlement in the interior of much of the Scottish Highlands. Argyll, however, gouged out by ice, flooded by the melt waters and deeply penetrated by sea lochs often twenty or more miles in length, was a soft target for Irish priests and Viking hordes alike. They sailed their boats the length of the sea lochs, carried them overland for the mile or two to the next sheet of water and thus worked their way far inland ignoring the wild impenetrable country on either bank. It was on the loch shores and along the river valleys that these newcomers chose to settle and it is here that we find the majority of today's villages.

The Scots have special names for their settlements, terms which are sometimes misunderstood by visitors. A township, for example, is not, as the name suggests, a town, but a group of houses standing together for a specific purpose. It might be an agricultural community sharing the runrigs of the ancient system of crofting or it might be home to servants of a big house, all working for and maintained by the heritor or landlord. In the days when clan culture was uppermost in the Highlands, lesser members of the clan lived in such townships supported by their laird and ready at a moment's notice to take up arms against his enemies. The term steading applies to the farm buildings often associated with a township or an individual farmhouse. Policies are the lands surrounding any substantial property.

Argyll was typical of counties of the western Highlands in being without towns until the eighteenth century. Places lacking sufficient population to be deemed a town might, however, assume importance because of their position as a base for legal or commercial activities. By the sixteenth century such settlements were being given the status of a burgh of barony. Inverary carried this title from the early days of the Earldom of Argyll, the Earl himself wielding the hand of justice throughout his domains. Oban was to become a burgh of barony but not until late in the eighteenth century.

The title of village, for the purposes of this book, refers to a settlement which is practically self-sufficient, undertaking many and varied activities and having amongst its population a variety of skills and professions, performing different services for the benefit of the community as a whole. By the end of the eighteenth century a village might expect to have a church, an inn or malt house, a school and a general store. There would almost certainly have been a blacksmith, a flesher (butcher), baker, tailor and cobbler. By the end of the nineteenth century one might add a post office to this list as well as a policeman. Not every small village had a doctor but there would almost certainly have been a midwife and possibly a village wise-woman practising the ancient arts of herbal medicine.

Few of Argyll's present-day villages date back to pre-Christian times although there are often Neolithic sites identified close by. Several were created to support Christian communities (kirktouns), for example Ardchattan on the north shore of Loch Etive and Clachan Seil in the parish of Kilbrandon. Dalmally, situated at a

Black house – a typical Highland dwelling until the late eighteenth century (*Author's Collection*)

major junction of routes through the Highlands had many reasons for its development but its early history suggests it was a shrine to St Conan who led a hermit's existence here and is said to have blessed the well, giving it healing properties. Pilgrims came from far and wide demanding food and shelter during their stay. Facilities built to provide these services became the foundations of the village.

By the middle of the fifteenth century each autumn saw an exodus of farm animals unlikely to survive a winter in the Highlands. One bull and a few good cows were housed in the black houses of the people, one half of the property being used as a byre. A ram and the best of the ewes were penned safely nearby. The remaining beasts were sent to market.

Every October from Oban to Stirling, from Mallaig to Crieff, from Craignish to Dumbarton, from the Outer Isles and from mainland Argyll, cattle and sheep were driven to the trysts (markets) and sold to provide meat for the burgeoning cities of the Lowlands. A small community entrusted its entire stock to a single drover and his team of men and dogs. Rarely did a drover pay outright for the animals he took to market but issued a promissory note underwritten by a bank, the forerunners of our present banknotes. So important was the trade in meat from the Highlands that successive Privy Councils from the reign of Queen Mary onwards, issued rules governing the activities of the drovers, restricting the tolls imposed upon users of roads through the Highlands and demanding suitable accommodation for the men and beasts as they made their way across country. On the assumption that a herd of cattle can be moved up to twelve miles in a day, stances or change-houses were established at intervals of between ten and twelve miles along the most popular routes. Those change-houses which were built by Royal Command were designated King's Houses, such as the inn near Bridge of Orchy. At first a drover's stance was merely required to provide grazing for beasts, food and shelter for men and dogs. As time went on a blacksmith became an essential member of the community. Even the cattle had to be shod to prevent damage to their hoofs from the stony tracks. Equally important was the cobbler who could make immediate repairs to the traveller's footware.

As the number of cattle movements increased annually, the stances came to depend more and more for supplies upon the local production of meat and dairy products, grain, root vegetables, ale and whisky. Whole communities grew up around the change-houses. As populations increased, there was a demand for a church and a school which were usually provided by the landowner who, in the case of much of north Argyll, was either the Duke of Argyll or the Earl of Breadalbane. A quick glance at the map will show that the villages of Tyndrum, Dalmally, Taynuilt and Connel are set at intervals of approximately ten miles, likewise Tyndrum, Bridge of Orchy, Glencoe and Inverlochy. The change-houses eventually gave way to inns and many of today's hotels rest upon the same foundations as those earlier examples of hospitality provision. Change-houses were also set up at all the major ferry points such as those at North and South Connel at the mouth of Loch Etive, and at Kilchrenan and Portsonachan on Loch Awe.

Both the Earls and Dukes of Argyll and the Earls and Marquesses of Breadalbane, who between them owned most of the county, were adept at exploiting the natural resources of their territory. The mountains were quarried for building stone, metal deposits, particularly lead were extracted from Glenorchy and Ardnamurchan, timber was taken from the forests and from the fourteenth century onwards the Slate Islands were quarried for their roofing slates. At first these enterprises were undertaken in order to build the personal dwellings of the clan chiefs and their people, Inveraray town and castle, for example, being constructed entirely from materials quarried on the Duke's own estates. By the seventeenth century, however, it became clear that there was money to be made selling the products of the quarries and mines both at home and abroad. Heavy materials could be shipped out by sea to anywhere in the world and as Scotsmen increasingly settled in far-flung places, they often demanded building materials from home in order to construct their churches and public buildings. This work increased to such an extent that it was necessary to bring in additional skilled labour, often from England as well as other parts of Scotland. Complete villages were constructed to house the workers and their families. At Easdale, slate was extracted to such an extent that at the peak of production in the mid-nineteenth century, 2,000 men, women and children were living in the slate villages of Lorn and surrounding lands. Above Strontian, the villages of Anaheilt, Scotstown and Ariundle mark the sites of eighteenth-century lead mines. In more recent times the Forestry Commission, in a major replanting programme during the 1950s, built an entire village at Dalavich and substantially increased the housing stock at such tiny settlements as Minard, Lochawe and Eredine, raising them to village status. The village of Dunbeg outside Oban was built from scratch in order to house civilian workers associated with naval operations in the Oban and Tobermory area during the Second World War. Kinlochleven was built to house workers in the aluminium-smelting industry which was introduced following the First World War. In the 1980s, the village of Craobh Haven was created specifically to meet the needs of holidaymakers.

One factor above all others which was to encourage settlement in the hinterland of Argyll was the coming of the railway in the latter years of the nineteenth century. Crianlarich, Tyndrum, Lochawe, Dalmally and Taynuilt became more readily available as holiday venues for those who had read and admired the journals of Queen Victoria and of such intrepid explorers as Dorothy Wordsworth and her brother William, James Boswell and Dr Samual Johnson, Thomas Pennant and Dean Munro. Now it was possible for a more comfort-loving society to experience real Highland grandeur from the corner seat of a first-class railway carriage and to fish the lochs and rivers by day while returning each night to a roaring fire, a good meal and a soft bed. When, nearly a century later, the roads were finally brought up to first-class standard, the villages were already well established alongside

Village of Craobh Haven, constructed with tourism in mind (*Author's Collection*)

the railway line. A road which required widening and straightening was diverted around the outskirts of the village.

With the exception of Ardnamurchan, Argyll shows little evidence of the Highland clearances. Very few villages were completely abandoned. Successive inheritors of the Argyll and Breadalbane titles concerned themselves with the provision of alternative employment introducing iron-smelting, gunpowder manufacture, linen-weaving and latterly aluminium-smelting using cheap hydroelectric power. Most of Argyll's settlements have survived into the twenty-first century and are ready to meet the challenge of Scotland's most important industry today – tourism.

1
LOCHGOILHEAD AND KILMORICH

*A stopover for kings and princes and a place where
travellers and pilgrims may rest and be thankful*

Archaeologists tell us that Stone Age people arrived from the east some 7,000 years ago to settle in Argyll. The oldest human remains in Argyll, dating from this period, have been found on the island of Jura but this does not necessarily suggest that the earliest settlers sailed around the coast of northern Scotland to get there. It is more likely that they made the hazardous but short sea crossing from mainland Argyll having moved across the land in their hunting and gathering forays. The most logical route for these earliest of settlers to have taken would have been along the valleys of the Rivers Forth and Clyde. Having found their way around Loch Lomond one must suppose they would have followed the game animals into the wild, mountainous lands to the west by way of the narrow neck of land which links Loch Lomond with the head of Loch Long.

On the outskirts of the village of Arrochar is the entrance to Glen Croe, one of the few land routes into the heart of Argyll. Today little

The Cobbler from Arrochar, 1910 (*Author's Collection*)

evidence exists here of the presence of prehistoric man but that is not to say that he did not shelter in the many caves to be found on these mountainsides when in pursuit of his quarry and leave behind those of his tribe that were killed in the chase, marking their presence by cairns and artefacts to take them into the after-life. He would surely have discovered the narrow pass through the hills which today we know as Glen Kinglas and found his way to the rich fishing grounds of Loch Fyne. There is abundant evidence to show that 5000 years BC there were people living on the western seaboard of Argyll but it is likely that for such settlers, just as today, Glen Croe was merely a means to an end. Those who came later to settle, to clear the land and farm it, chose the coastal areas to the west, the river valleys and the loch shores where there was a constant supply of fish for food, even when game became scarce. The lochs also provided access by water to other settlements for trading purposes and by building their more permanent shelters on islands in the lochs these early peoples could live safe from wild beasts and marauding neighbours. Where there were no suitable islands, they created them, felling trees and piling on rocks to give such a stable foundation that several examples of these crannogs, or artifical islands, can be seen throughout Argyll.

The earliest settlement took place in this area at the head of Loch Goil and also at the head of Loch Fyne. The most important settlement, Lochgoilhead, is recorded in the Hearth Tax schedule of 1693 as a kirktoun. No one saint has been named as its founder but the earliest records show that the first church built here was attributed to three Christian Brothers and the name, the Church of the Three Holy Brethren, was recorded in the registers of the Synod of Argyll in the fourteenth century.

When priests from Ireland began their mission to convert the Picts to Christianity in the sixth century AD, it was common practice for them to build their cells or places of worship close to earlier settlements at some spot where the local population was accustomed to worshiping its pagan gods. One may therefore suppose that a settlement of some kind preceded that of the Brothers, probably by some hundreds of years.

From the earliest records of parish boundaries, Lochgoilhead has always been described as the parish church although at Clachan, at the head of Loch Fyne, another church, Kilmorich, of medieval origin, also enjoyed similar status. Eventually the two parishes merged but because of the distance between them and the difficulty of travelling the dangerous roads, particularly in winter, both churches were considered to be parish churches. Nevertheless Lochgoilhead was regarded as the administrative centre of the parish and as time went on it became also the centre for education and other public services.

Originally of simple longitudinal plan, Lochgoilhead church today retains some masonry of fourteenth-century origin, in particular the walling to the east and west aisles. Much of the building, however, has been remodelled over the centuries. The Campbells of Ardkinglas, a branch of the Campbell family of Lochawe, who held title to these lands from the thirteenth century, are commemorated here. The most eye-catching monument to be retained is the late sixteenth-century Ardkinglas arch in the centre of which is a doorway, now blocked. This elaborate portico once led into the Ardkinglas aisle where the family were buried. Unfortunately, during reconstruction work in the nineteenth century, it was found necessary to demolish the burial aisle and the monumental stones were removed.

The north aisle owes its origin to remodelling in the eighteenth century which also accounted for the inclusion of two tall round-arched windows on either side of the pulpit on the south wall. Two galleries were introduced early in the nineteenth century but today only the Drimsynie loft on the west wall remains. A session house was added to the south wall in 1832 with a distinctive pyramid roof topped with a birdcage belfry. In 1894 Campbell Douglas added a porch to the north wall.

The major alterations of 1832 came at an unfortunate time for the Church of Scotland. From the Reformation, the Church in Scotland had embraced Presbyterianism, and adherents to the Church of Rome were barely tolerated. The Church was governed, as it is today, by the General Assembly under the leadership of its Moderator. Unfortunately, having no money of its own, the Church of Scotland was beholden to the local landowners, or heritors, for financial support for its ministers, its schools, for church buildings and for the relief of the poor. Over time, this gave an inordinate amount of power to the secular arm of the State, the men holding the purse-strings. It also opened the way to a form of patronage which in some cases included corruption and nepotism on a grand scale.

Believing that the Church belonged only to the true Christ and to no one else, many ministers and their parishioners rebelled against the system of patronage, breaking away to form the Free Church of Scotland in what became known as the Disruption of 1843.

Many parishioners of Lochgoilhead were party to this rebellion. Without a church building, they were obliged to meet for worship in their own homes, in the fields or wherever they could find shelter in which to hold their services. It was not until 1883 that Free Church members were in a position to build their own church in the village. Of traditional Gothic design, the building remained in use as a place of worship until 1952. For some years it was used as a community hall but in recent times has been boarded up and abandoned.

Other buildings in the village help to trace its history from a small rural township to a bustling tourist centre in the mid-nineteenth century, a position from which it has now largely retreated having been overtaken by the huge development of holiday accommodation and leisure facilities on the opposite shore of the loch at Drimsynie.

The inn, now the Lochgoilhead Hotel, dates from the eighteenth century but almost certainly occupies the foundations of a much earlier establishment. This end of the loch was always a suitable site for the embarkation and disembarkation of travellers and while they waited for transport for the next stage of a journey, some form of accommodation would have been necessary. Pilgrims journeying to Iona Abbey and Ardchattan Priory and visitors to the Campbell strongholds at Kilchurn and Inveraray, would undoubtedly have used the Clyde waterway, disembarking at this point to take the short cut through the mountains to Loch Fyne.

With the coming of pleasure-steamers from Glasgow, Lochgoilhead, by the 1860s, had become a favoured tourist centre. Towards the end of the century, wealthy businessmen built their weekend retreats here and came to retire. The shoreline is dotted with late Victorian villas often built by their owners in the style of some earlier venture abroad so that Swiss chalet rubs shoulders with baronial castle and Tudor manor house. The fine ironwork on a house called Alma suggests a visit to Spain, while Burnknowe is reminiscent of Italy. Towards the end of the nineteenth century many of these substantial houses took in paying guests, fulfilling a growing need for holiday accommodation. The village population remained fairly static during the early years of the twentieth century, its popularity as a holiday centre increased by the acquisition of a vast tract of land to the north-east of the village, the Ardgour estate. This was presented to the people of Glasgow by the owner, Lord Rowallan, an ardent supporter of the work of Lord Baden-Powell and his successor as Chief Scout. The YMCA (Glasgow) built accommodation for campers in 1910 and since then, thousands of young people from Lowland Scotland, all parts of the British Isles and abroad, have come here each year to enjoy the countryside and the many outdoor activities offered by mountain and loch.

There are few records of the inhabitants of Lochgoilhead but the 1879 obituary to Neil Campbell tells us something of the times. Neil was resident in the village for twenty-five years and for much of that period he ran the village shop and was the postmaster. He was brought up on his parents' farm at Drymayinsbeg, was a good scholar and attended university, where he was reading for the Ministry. His studies were interrupted by the death of his father and he returned to run the family farm, eventually becoming the village merchant in the 1850s. During the pastorates of Dr MacDougall and Mr McCorkindale, Neil was an elder of the Kirk and an active supporter of the local Conservative Member of Parliament, Colonel Malcolm.

Neil Campbell was also a member of the Volunteer Force, the Argyllshire Highland Rifles, raised under the umbrella of the Argylls during the 1860s. The Volunteers were local militia recruited in support of a national army whose resources had been stretched to the limit by Britain's Empire-building activities. Invasion by the French when Britain was in such a vulnerable situation, had become a real possibility and these Volunteer companies were raised throughout Scotland. Equipped, for the most part, with weaponry dating from the Peninsular Wars, the provision of suitable uniforms was dependent upon the largess of the local aristocracy, in this case the Duke of Argyll. Many fine marksmen were discovered in the ranks of the Volunteers, some of them having been gamekeepers or perhaps even poachers. Although the French threat came to nothing, a force of Volunteers fought in South Africa alongside the regular troops, during the Boer War.

Another character to spend time amongst the people of this remote Highland village was John MacIntyre who became known through his writing as 'John Brandane'. John was born in Rothesay and as a boy was put to work in a Glasgow cotton mill. By dint of his own determination and self-education he raised himself to the position of warehouse clerk. Further study at evening classes equipped him with the necessary qualifications to enter Glasgow University as a student of medicine. He graduated in 1901 and after a spell as surgeon at Glasgow Infirmary where he met O.H. Mavor (James Bridie) he himself became interested in writing. Having spent the first World War on the Western Front, John became Medical Officer of Health

Horses used to haul timber, *c.* 1930s (*copyright © RCAHMS*)

at Lochgoilhead. It was here that he began his new career, filling every spare minute in writing for the theatre so that by the time he moved on to another medical practice on Mull, he was in a position to become a founder member, in 1922, of the Scottish National Players for whom he wrote his best-known work, *The Glen is Mine*.

Although this part of Argyll was never subject to the nineteenth-century clearances brought about by the introduction of sheep farming, the parish was to experience a steady decline in population during the early part of the twentieth century when the steamers ceased to be an attractive form of transport and tourists were lured away to other resorts by train and motor car. The decline in population was halted in the 1940s when the Ministry of Defence took over the sea lochs for various training activities of the combined land and sea forces. Military establishments, set up overnight, created the need for additional accommodation. A number of houses were built on the east and south sides of the village and the population almost doubled in a short space of time. This, of course underlined a need for improved infrastructure, and put pressure on schools and other public services. The additional employment opportunities which were generated encouraged further newcomers to the area. In 1945, the withdrawal of the military was by no means immediate but as army and navy personnel began to move out, their place was taken by those introduced by the Forestry Commission who were initiating a major programme of planting. This activity has continued, although with modern, sophisticated equipment there are fewer opportunities for employment.

While some jobs have dwindled over the years, the rise in interest in water sports and outdoor activities of all kinds has brought a different type of work to the locality. Small businesses concerned with fishing, boating and other water-based activities have grown up along the loch shore. Many of the large old villas still accommodate visitors during the summer season. There have been few changes to the facilities offered by the village in recent years. One very large, ugly concrete construction, built initially by the military, has become a general store providing the immediate requirements of the neighbourhood while the original village shop and post office, to all appearances little changed from Neil Campbell's time, sits alongside it. The quay, once the scene of so much activity with steamers bringing in goods and visitors, has become no more than a convenient parking place for the occasional day visitor.

Across the water, the Drimsynie complex of chalets and caravans with its own shops, swimming pool and leisure facilities, appears to intimidate the villagers of Lochgoilhead. This is a pity because there is potential to offer a pleasant, village-based attraction for those taking their holidays at Drimsynie which, so far, has been largely neglected.

Village life is full. According to the regular and excellent reporting by their local correspondent to the *Oban Times*, many social events are initiated by the various clubs and organisations. The parish church and the school are centres for much of this activity but the community hall, built in 1898 by James Salmon & Son, is still in use. Despite ugly mid-twentieth-century roughcast and an inappropriately slated roof in place of wooden shingles, the original veranda and gables allow us to imagine how it looked when it was built, in the English Arts and Crafts style of the late nineteenth century. Repair and reconstruction, with a return to the spirit of the original building, must surely be worth consideration.

If Lochgoilhead is to be considered a kirktoun then surely Carrick, situated a few miles down the loch on its western shore, is a castletoun. A castle is first mentioned at this place in connection with Thomas Bruce, whose family constituted a sept of Clan Campbell. As Earl of Carrick, he formed an alliance – *Carryke, Kyle and Cunninghame against the oppressive rule of the English* – in 1312 which resulted in the fierce battles between Edward I of England and the Scottish Lords. Thomas Bruce was succeeded by his son, Robert, who became King Robert I. By the treaty of Edinburgh and Northampton, the Pope granted to the Scottish Crown the privilege of anointment and it was Robert's son, David, who as King David II was the first of the Scottish kings to be crowned in this manner at Scone, in 1328. The very close alliance between the Clan Campbell and the Scottish Crown carried over to the British Crown after 1603. With very few exceptions, the Campbells have supported the reigning monarch ever since, often angering more belligerent Highland neighbours who regarded the Campbells as traitors for toadying to the English even when the monarch happened to be Scottish! In recognition of their loyalty, both the Earls and Dukes of Argyll and their cousins, the Earls of Breadalbane, were many times awarded lands and titles confiscated from dissident lairds. As a result both sides of the family became rich and powerful.

The present castle at Carrick was built as a stronghold in the late fourteenth century, by the Loch Awe Campbells who later became the Earls and later, Dukes of Argyll. Carrick proved to be a convenient overnight stop on the way north. Sir Colin Campbell of Glenorchy who became the first Earl of Argyll granted the lands between Loch Fyne and Loch Long and the captaincy of Carrick Castle to a kinsman who thereafter took the name of Campbell of Ardkinglas. Both the castle and the territory associated with it remained in the hands of the same family until the nineteenth century. The castle itself, however, was fired by the Duke of Atholl as punishment for the 9th Earl of Argyll, the only member of his family to support the opposition to the Crown, during the rebellion of 1685. Argyll was subsequently beheaded in Edinburgh.

The most notable of guests to stay at Carrick Castle was Queen Mary I but it was often used by the Duke himself and by his visitors. At times it was used as a secure prison and on occasion housed a garrison of troops. For several generations it was used as the dower-house for widowed duchesses. On the second floor of the building, which was divided into three apartments, was the library where all the important documents relating to the Earl's estates were housed. Here, too, was the treasury, the castle at Inverary being thought too vulnerable to attack.

Carrick Castle in 2003 (*Author's Collection*)

Carrick Castle stands upon a rocky promontory sticking out into the loch and surrounded on three sides by deep water. The oblong structure, almost a double square, rises to fifteen metres above the level of its foundation. The three storeys are connected by stairs built into the external walls and the interior is lit by randomly placed windows of different age, decoration and dimension. In the early seventeenth century additional buildings were provided on the east side, facing the loch. These seem to have been used as kitchens, guard-house and stores. Following the deliberate destruction of the interior by fire in 1685, the building was left untouched for two centuries but in the early 1900s partial repairs were carried out. In 1988 the castle was bought by architect Ian Begg who created living accommodation on the first and second floors under a steeply pitched, slated roof. Depending upon the final use to which the castle may be put, its repair could trigger an improvement in the economy of the adjoining village which has grown up around it since the beginning of the thirteenth century.

In the early days the village would have housed the servants employed both in the castle and on the Ardkinglas estate. One can well imagine the presence here of blacksmith, tailor, bootmaker and baker together with foresters and gamekeepers, fishermen and boatmen to ferry people back and forth across the loch. With the destruction of the castle in the late seventeenth century, there was little encouragement to maintain a village of any kind so it is to the credit of the generations who came after that they were able to glean a living from the area.

The houses, mainly of eighteenth- and nineteenth-century origin, are built around three sides of a square in the middle of which stands a multi-storey rectangular tenement block called Hillside, built in 1877. Set against a background of single-storey cottages of local stone, this huge red-sandstone construction appears completely out of place. It is as though some gigantic helicopter had picked it up out of the back streets of Glasgow and set it down here amidst mountain scenery. Its age suggests that Hillside was built to fulfil an urgent need for additional accommodation connected with the growing tourism of that date. The rest of the buildings vary in age from eighteenth-century farm-workers' cottages to twentieth-century prefabricated structures, some of which are attributable to the Ministry of Defence. There is nothing to mitigate against the general drabness of the place except for a group of Victorian villas built alongside the shore road. These speak of better days when the wooden jetty beside the castle, built of timber in 1877, encouraged the steamers from Glasgow to pull in here and set down those of their passengers who preferred to walk the last few miles beside the water to Lochgoilhead. No doubt at that time the various cottages would have provided refreshment, even a bed for the night for weary visitors, but today only the single-storey stone building which is the village pub provides for the few visitors who come here, lured by the name and the historic reference. The school is closed. The only place of worship is the parish church at the head of the loch.

In 1945 the old timber pier which served the village was demolished and a concrete jetty, built by the Ministry of Defence, took its place. This is firmly padlocked and shrouded in warning notices discouraging its use by the boating fraternity. Like Lochgoilhead, this is a place with potential for tourism but one which remains to be exploited.

In its position as the administrative centre of the parish, Lochgoilhead demanded good communications with other villages within its orbit. While these were always available by water, the voyage around the Isle of Bute to Inveraray was long and hazardous.

Edinburgh Castle approaching Carrick pier, 1912 (*Author's Collection*)

From earliest times two overland routes were established, the first following the valley of the River Goil, rising steeply to meet the route through Glen Croe and Glen Kinglas at the highest point of the pass. The shorter and more direct road connected Lochgoilhead and Carrick Castle through the narrow pass of Glen Bean with the village of St Catherines situated on Loch Fyneside, opposite the town of Inveraray. Glen Beag, at one time apparently favoured by outlaws and cattle rustlers, is widely recognised as Hell's Glen, although the only recorded attack of any kind took place in the twentieth century when a travelling bank was waylaid, the guards overcome and the contents stolen.

This was the route normally taken by the earl and his entourage, parties visiting the castle at Inverary being closely guarded by Argyll's soldiers. Over the centuries the road became less hazardous, was properly metalled and chosen as the most appropriate route for public transportation of passengers to and from Inverary. Thomas Pennant, Boswell and Johnson, and Saint-Just, those intrepid travellers of the late eighteenth century, all mention their passage through the glen in the accounts of their travels through the Highlands. In the 1821 edition of the *Principal Pleasure Tours in Scotland*, the route through Glen Beag is advocated. Many travellers of the early nineteenth century make reference to the coachman, John Campbell, who was also proprietor of the St Catherines Inn.

Horse-drawn coach employed in the 1880s (*Easdale Museum*)

Coachy Jock, as he was known, was a raconteur of great wit who regaled his passengers with all manner of tall tales about the ride through the glen. He it was who coined the name Hell's Glen. In order to provide his horses with water when they reached the highest section of the pass, John built a trough on the side of the road at a spot where a convenient burn could be diverted through a pipe in order to fill it. The pipe emerged from between the rocks so unobtrusively that it appeared as though the water was springing from the rocks themselves. With obvious biblical reference, John called it Moses' Well! Such a popular fellow received generous tips from many of his passengers. These he saved towards the building of a school at St Catherines. His generosity was acknowledged in a document in a bottle, placed in the foundations during the building. Because the school also provided for the children from small townships further along the loch, a special jetty was built for the use of those who rowed themselves along the loch to school and back, every day. Towards the end of the twentieth century the school closed for lack of pupils, those children remaining in the village being bussed daily to larger establishments elsewhere. John Campbell's school remains in use as a meeting place for villagers but its little jetty has long since disappeared.

The Tourists' Guide for 1878 refers to a 'large well-appointed coach serving Loch Goilhead and St Catherines whence the steamer *Fairy* sails for Inveraray'.

Throughout recorded history, St Catherines was a ferry terminal and the village grew from its beginnings as a drover's stance during the seventeenth century. From the days of Queen Mary when the Privy Council first laid down the rules by which drovers should conduct their activities across Scotland, Inverary to St Catherines was an important ferry crossing and even after the new Military Road was constructed following the 1745 Rising, cattle and sheep were still ferried across the loch in flat-bottomed barges thereby cutting off a five-mile journey around the head of Loch Fyne.

Over the years, the ferries changed from sailing ships and barges to coal-fired steamers. One of the most notable of these was *The Fairy*, a paddle steamer purchased by Inveraray town council in 1893. Her captain was Duncan Bell, her pilot, Donuil Dubh and her engineer, Shon Gillies. The crew was Dugal Piobair. Sounding as though they might have stepped straight out of a Neil Munro story, these were well-loved characters on both sides of the water and it is said that on a Sunday, when alcoholic liquor could be sold only to bona fide travellers, the men of Inveraray would board the ferry to travel to St Catherines Inn where, in company with the crew, they might legitimately consume quantities of the uisge beatha. One can well imagine the merry trip back across the loch, later in the day!

In 1963 the St Catherines–Inveraray ferry was discontinued. The old ferry landing remains and for a short time during the 1980s a ferry service was revived. After a summer season during which the ferry was poorly supported it was withdrawn.

As was the case with all drovers' stances, to the need for basic accommodation were added other services required by the travellers – an ale house, tobacco, food supplies and clothing together with grazing land for the beasts, were provided by the villagers. The drovers were well paid and the rates charged for a night's lodging and for grazing the herds, although laid down by statute, were not ungenerous. St Catherines prospered as a village well into the nineteenth century, by which time cattle began to be moved by train and steamer rather than being walked for hundreds of miles across the Highlands.

In the 1880s, visited now by the Clyde pleasure steamers, the village had become a favoured venue for family holidays and for retirement.

Early worker's cottages, built of stone rubble, harled and whitewashed under a slated roof, were joined by late Victorian villas, some of which offered accommodation for visitors, while others were second homes for the better-off city gentlemen and their families.

From earliest times the villagers of St Catherines and smaller settlements along the loch had attended church at Clachan at the head of the loch, many being obliged to travel by boat. The parish church of Kilmorich was of fourteenth-century origin although a far more ancient cell created by an Irish saint of that name had existed previously on the same site, parishioners coming from Glen Fyne and Glen Shira as well as from the eastern shore of the loch. Today there is little sign that a village existed here in the past. Of the medieval church of Kilmorich, only the burial ground remains, the headstones for the most part indecipherable. A short way from the burial ground a rudely carved cross stands on a low mound. It is said that the people of Glen Shira erected this to mark the spot from which they first caught sight of their destination, as they made their way to worship in the old church. Today, a number of modern houses and some prosperous small businesses are evidence of a growing community of enterprising folk so perhaps this is, once more, a village in the making.

In 1816 the medieval parish church was abandoned and its successor was built at Cairndow, at the entrance to Glen Kinglas.

The village of Cairndow grew up in support of the fourteenth-century fortified tower house of the Campbells of Ardkinglas. By the end of the seventeenth century, Ardkinglas Castle was a ruin. Plans were made at that time to build a suitable residence in the grounds but it was another one hundred years before a seven-bay mansion was completed in 1795. The family lived here until 1831 when the house burnt down. A block of eighteenth-century stables was converted into living accommodation for the family during the reconstruction of the destroyed building. Over a period of years several notable architects were invited to submit plans but family fortunes were failing and eventually the estate was sold with only the converted stable block as residence. During the first decade of the twentieth century the new owner, Sir Andrew Noble, commissioned the architect Sir Robert Lorimer to build a new mansion.

The present Ardkinglas House is a complex mixture of styles with crowstep-gabled roofs of differing heights and typically Lorimer-style pedimented eaves dormers. A pair of bell roofs accentuate the flanks while a tall cap house tower with a cone-shaped top rises above the remainder of the roofs. The interior is a magnificent conglomeration of many styles and periods, more classical than medieval in approach. The simpler architecture of the Old Ardkinglas House, the converted stables, is regarded more sympathetically by modern-day critics but the crowning glory of the estate is its walled garden of early nineteenth-century origin and the very fine arboretum in the valley of the Kinglas water.

On the boundary of the parish with that of Inveraray, across the bay, lies Dunderave Castle, occupying a promontory of rock which gives it a commanding and almost impregnable position. This was the seat of the chief of Clan Macnachten (MacNaughton) who originally occupied a much earlier castle in Glen Shira. Built *c.* 1598 it consists of the original tower house with a circular turnpike stair. Having fallen into ruin by the end of the nineteenth century it was largely remodelled and restored by Sir Robert Lorimer.

A tragic story attaches to the Macnachten family and the castle. John, the last chief of the Macnachtens, fell in love with the second of the eight daughters of Campbell of Ardkinglas. Anxious to dispose first of his eldest and plainer daughter, Campbell decided that she should be the bride and bullied his younger daughter into submission. It was customary before the marriage for the bride to wear a thick veil, hiding her features from her future husband. The ceremony completed, the married couple were carried off to their nuptial chamber. Besotted with wine and unable to see clearly in the ill-lit room, the groom was unaware that a switch had been made and the marriage which was consummated that night was to the wrong sister! After a furious quarrel during which Campbell indicated that he saw nothing wrong, swearing that the older sister would make just as good a wife and decreed that in any case it was only right that the eldest be married off first, Macnachten agreed to make a go of it. When the first child of the union was born it was the second sister who attended Macnachten's wife. The old love was rekindled and the thwarted lovers, no longer willing to accept the consequences of Campbell's trick, absconded to Ireland where they lived without benefit of wedding vows for the rest of their lives.

In 1803, Dorothy Wordsworth and her brother William set out from Arrochar after two o'clock in the afternoon, hoping to reach Cairndow

Rest and Be Thankful stone, Glen Croe (*Author's Collection*)

by sundown. In their little two-wheeled carriages pulled by a small pony, they took the new military road up Glen Croe to the head of the pass and in so doing, Dorothy observed a single farm and its steadings. The buildings she describes still exist in much the same form today. It was the only habitation they saw on their journey.

At the head of the pass some mason, a soldier of General Wade's 1748 company of engineers, relieved no doubt to have reached the highest contour in their road-making, carved a stone inviting travellers to Rest and Be Thankful. Information added at a later date records that the road was repaired in 1765 by the 93rd regiment and transferred to the Commissioners for H. R. and B (harbours, roads and public buildings?) in the year 1814. Despite the re-routing of this major trunk road in the last half of the twentieth century, taking a wider, straighter path along the side of the glen, the name Rest and Be Thankful still applies, although the old stone which is in its original position, now stands alongside a modern car-park.

Glancing back along the road to Arrochar, one can still make out the old military road (now a cycle track) which Dorothy and her

Font – probably from Kilmorlich Parish Church (*Author's Collection*)

brother took and the steep approach to the top of the pass which so fatigued their pony.

The sun went down as Dorothy and William descended into Glen Kinglas and she speaks in glowing terms of the ruby-red colouring of the western sky which she saw reflected in the waters of the tarn at the head of the glen. It was quite dark when they reached the inn at Cairndow where the hostess lit a fire especially for them and provided an excellent meal. Today this same journey can be completed in under an hour but it is unlikely that the motorist, straining to pass some slow lorry, heavily laden with felled tree trunks, ever has time to witness the glories of the landscape as described by Dorothy.

The Cairndow parish church of Kilmorich was built in 1816 to replace the medieval church at Clachan. In the porch, which is sited beneath the square tower, is part of an ancient baptismal font bearing graffiti including a sketch of an old Highland birlinner galley. Removed from the ruins of the original parish church for safe-keeping towards the end of the eighteenth century, this was discovered in a

Cairndow Parish Church (*Author's Collection*)

heap of masonry in the grounds of Inverary Castle and restored to the Cairndow parish church in the 1990s.

Behind the square tower the body of the building is octagonal, the design reminiscent of that at Dalmally. The walls are of masonry blocks and rubble infill, harled and whitewashed, the pyramidal roof slated. The pointed arched windows are edged with contrasting sandstone. A small gallery, the Ardkinglas loft, is entered from the tower. The tombstones in the surrounding churchyard date only from the time of construction but there is an older burial ground close by.

The village is a modest run of houses arranged along a narrow strip of flat ground beside the loch. The oldest of these is the eighteenth-century inn, mentioned by Dorothy Wordsworth. The building retains few of its original features, having been extended several times over the years. The possibility of commuting to work by road, together with the increased ability of people to work from their own homes, linked to the Internet, resulted in a demand for additional accommodation towards the end of the twentieth century. This has been met by the erection of a few houses of local traditional design and, close to the church, a small development of modestly dormered houses designed by John Boys.

Cairndow village is a quiet place with few claims to an exciting history. Although the village grew up in association with Ardkinglas Castle there is little doubt that the original inn was a drovers' stance. The road through Glen Kinglas was a drove road to the Crieff and Dumbarton trysts. The economy was much improved in the years following the Jacobite Rising of 1745 when the new military road and the many bridges involved were constructed by Wade's troops. At the time hundreds of men were stationed in the surrounding glens, their only entertainment being the village inn.

Like St Catherines, Cairndow has always been associated with ferries and with steamer traffic and during the nineteenth century the village became dependent upon tourism. During the Second World War the village was invaded by the military once again when the combined sea and land forces of the Allies, and particularly units of the Special Forces, came here for training. The Duke of Argyll entertained many important figures associated with the war including Lord Louis Mountbatten, Sir Winston Churchill and King Haakon of Norway whose men trained here for their clandestine activities in occupied Norway. Older villagers recall the visits of some of these personalities with considerable pride.

2

THE ROYAL BURGH OF INVERARAY

Campbell earls, dukes and palaces,
Loch Fyne kippers and prime Scotch beef

The parish of Inveraray includes a narrow strip of land about fifteen miles long fronting the shores of Loch Fyne together with three glens, drained by the Rivers Aray, Shira and Fyne, all of which enter the loch at its north-eastern end. Until the sixteenth century the parish was known as Kilmalieu, a name which has been retained only for the burial ground which stands beside the main road to Glasgow, beyond the Aray Bridge.

Chambered cairns, scattered below the ridge of hills bordering the narrow coastal plain, are evidence of Man's occupation from Neolithic times. The fertile alluvial deposits forming the banks of the three meandering rivers provided excellent grazing and encouraged early farmers to settle here. Access to neighbouring settlements by water made trading possible and sea fishing provided adequate food supplies when game was scarce.

Eventually the sea loch was to invite exploration by at least one Irish priest who came to this location during the sixth century and built his cell. The prefix Kil- refers to the cell, in this case of a priest called Malieu (although this may be a corruption of some other name.)

The early village probably grew up around the priest's cell and the medieval church which succeeded it. All that remains of the latter is the Kilmalieu burial ground, a new parish church having been built in the centre of the new town of Inverary in the eighteenth century. The mercat cross which now stands by the loch, close to the war memorial, has late medieval tracery suggesting an origin in Kintyre or Iona. It is believed to have stood beside the old parish church and was probably transported from the old town at the time of the reconstruction.

By 1432, Sir Colin Campbell of Lochawe had built a Campbell stronghold on Loch Fyne, calling it Inveraray ('the mouth of the River Aray'). Although he had already built an imposing castle at Kilchurn at the head of Loch Awe, Sir Colin had recognised the trading potential of Inveraray and determined to make it the main seat of Clan Campbell. Not only was Inveraray to become the only market town in Argyll outside Kintyre but for centuries it was also the administrative centre and seat of justice for the county. Not unsurprisingly it remains to this day the principal residence of the Duke of Argyll.

The earliest Campbell chieftain on record is Sir Colin Campbell (Cailean Mor – the great Colin) whose original stronghold was on the island of Innis Chonnell in Loch Awe. By the Charter of 1315, granted by King Robert I, Colin took the title Sir Colin Campbell of Lochawe as these extracts from a facsimile in Anderson's Diploma illustrates:

> Robert by the grace of God King of Scots, to all good men of his whole land, greeting. Know ye that we have given, granted and by our present charter confirmed to our beloved and faithful Sir Colin, son of Neil Cambel, for his homage and service, the whole land of Louchaw and the land of Ardscodyrthe, with the pertinents: to be held and had by Sir Colin and his heirs of us and our heirs in fee and heritage and in a fee barony by all their right bounds and marches . . . the said Colin and his heirs providing for us and our heirs, in return for the said lands, one ship of forty oars in our service with all its pertinents and sufficient men at the expense of the same Sir Colin and his heirs, for forty days as often as they shall be forwarned.

Colin's reward was for supporting Robert Bruce in his successful bid for the throne of Scotland. When Bruce defeated the MacDougall Lords of Lorne he confiscated their stronghold, Dunstaffnage Castle, placing a Campbell in charge. To this day the Captaincy of the castle is held by a Campbell.

This was the first in a long chain of events which were to bring lands, wealth and subsequently great power to the clan whose chieftains became the Earls and later the Dukes, of Argyll. Always closely allied with the monarchy and generally a powerful voice in the land, the prospects of Clan Campbell were greatly enhanced during the sixteenth century when, as Chancellor to King James IV, the 2nd Earl of Argyll was given charge of the resettlement of lands forfeited by Macdonald, the Lord of the Isles. Argyll was quick to allocate these tenancies to his own kinsmen, thus gaining overall control of a vast territory from the Mull of Kintyre to Ardnamurchan. In combination with the lands held by Argyll's cousins, the Breadalbane Campbells of Glenorchy, the Campbell holdings now stretched inland as far as Stirlingshire and Perthshire.

The 2nd Earl had scarcely completed his task of reallocating the tenancies, however, when he was killed alongside his monarch at the battle of Flodden in 1513. The outlying agents, kinsmen appointed by the Earl of Argyll, took the names of the territory over which they had control: Campbell of Kinglas; Campbell of Dunstaffnage; Campbell of Lochnell; and so on. Without an occupying army to support them, these were simply a band of middle managers placed in charge of sub-tenants, cottars and servants who had been loyal kinsmen and supporters of the deposed Lord of the Isles. The Campbell overlords were answerable to their Chief but dependent upon the goodwill of the local population. When interests clashed, the local overseer was as likely as not to turn a blind eye and even the Clan Chieftain knew when to let things ride. This avoidance of conflict kept the Campbells in power for centuries. Only once did they transgress.

At the Reformation which had taken place in Scotland during the second quarter of the sixteenth century, Archibald Campbell, the 5th Earl of Argyll, embraced the Presbyterian religion and retained favour with the Crown. As a consequence, when Charles I was executed in 1649, the 8th Earl and 1st Marquess of Argyll refused support for Montrose's efforts to place the Catholic Charles II on the Scottish throne. A less warlike figure than many of his ancestors, Argyll fled Inveraray Castle with his immediate family as Montrose's men marched into Glen Shira. Later, while fighting in support of the English at the battle of Inverlochy, Argyll's men suffered enormous losses. Once again their chief lost his nerve and deserted them at the height of the battle. Thereafter, until the succession of the next earl, clan loyalties were severely strained.

When Charles II was eventually restored to the English throne, one of his first acts was to have the 8th Earl executed for treason. His son, the 9th Earl, being a practising Catholic, was allowed to succeed to the title but then, in 1689, when the English removed James II (VII of Scotland) from the throne, the Earl of Argyll fled to the Low Countries with Monmouth where they plotted to restore the Catholic monarch to his throne.

For this act of treachery Argyll was exiled and eventually lost his life. At a time when Judge Jeffries was wielding a terrible revenge against the Catholics in England, Scotland's Privy Council attacked the Scottish rebels with even greater fervour. The Marquess of Atholl was instructed to:

Destroy what you can to all who joined in any manner of way with Argyll. All . . . who are not come off on your or Breadalbane's advertisement are to be killed or disabled from ever fighting again; and burn all the houses except honest men's, and destroy Inveraray and all the castles and what you cannot undertake leave to those who come after you . . . Let the women and children be transported to remote islands . . .

Some Campbell lairds were hanged, some exiled, but most escaped, largely due to the incompetence of Atholl himself who very soon tired of his duties in Argyll. When King William ascended the throne there was a general amnesty and the 10th Earl, Archibald, was created 1st Duke of Argyll. During the Jacobite risings which followed, the Argylls remained firmly on the side of the Crown and strong supporters of Unionism.

In 1746, once again an Argyll, this time Archibald Campbell, the 3rd Duke, was given responsibility for the redistribution of lands forfeited by the Jacobites. Now Argyll and Breadalbane between them controlled the entire county. The Campbell family did not reach the peak of its power however until, in 1871, John Douglas Sutherland, Marquess of Lorne and later to become the 9th Duke of Argyll, married Princess Louise, the daughter of Queen Victoria.

Following the accession of the 3rd Duke of Argyll, there was a period of relative calm when Archibald could consider an elaborate plan to transform his estates into models of neatness and efficiency. Included in the scheme were a new town at Inveraray, a new castle and a series of model farms.

By the middle of the eighteenth century, Sir Colin Campbell's original castle had fallen into ruin and the castletoun which had grown up under its walls was a cluttered mass of buildings which, although individually having a certain charm, offended the tidy mind of the new incumbent and, apparently, the nose of the Duchess!

The old town of Inveraray could boast a tolbooth, two schools, a church offering services in both Gaelic and English and a number of stone built, slated, town houses. When in 1745 the 3rd Duke commissioned Roger Morris to design a new castle, the architect was also invited to submit plans for a complete new town. The existing buildings were to be demolished and the site of the new town was set well away from the castle on a promontory on the opposite shore of the bay. William Adam, succeeded upon his death in 1748 by his son John, was responsible for supervising the work.

At about the time Argyll was designing his scheme for Inveraray,

General Wade submitted his own plans for a military road linking Dumbarton with Dalmally and Fort William. On seeing Wade's plan, Argyll realised that in driving through Glen Aray, the road would pass right under the walls of his new castle. Without giving the real reason, the influential Duke managed to persuade the Commissioners for Roads to begin their work from the Dumbarton end. By the time the road reached Inveraray, the castle was already well under construction and Argyll was able to insist that Wade reroute his road giving the castle a wide berth.

By the time of the 3rd Duke's death in 1761, the castle was nearly finished but work on the town had hardly begun. The old town had been demolished and temporary accommodation erected to house those displaced. There was considerable resentment on the part of the local population, among the most vociferous of objectors being MacCorquodale who kept the inn at the edge of the old town.

'If I must go,' he declared, 'I shall make sure my descendants will know that once we lived here and were happy.'

He took an iron pot and a pan from his kitchen and while working as a mason on the outer wall surrounding the castle grounds, he incorporated them in the stonework. Both objects remained in full view of passing traffic until the 1940s when it is suggested, US servicemen stole the pan as a souvenir. The pot remains in situ to this day.

When Archibald Campbell died in 1761 his cousin, Major-General John Campbell, became the 4th Duke of Argyll. Although not much interested in the changes started by his cousin, the soldier Duke allowed work to continue on rebuilding the castle, Robert Mylne being engaged to change the main entrance from the south-west front to the north-east. Work on the town and surrounds was set aside until the 4th Duke's death in 1770.

Inveraray Castle has received mixed reactions from architectural critics over the years. Built within a broad shallow fosse the building is a rectangle seven bays by five with a round tower at each of the four corners. Battlements were more for decoration than intended usefulness and indeed there was never any need to defend the castle from attack. A central square tower dominates the four outer walls. This contains a galleried hall lit by large pointed-arch windows. The fosse is crossed on the north-east side by a double-arched bridge making a grand entry to the building. Following a fire in 1877, Anthony Salvin was commissioned to restore the interior and to raise the main

Inveraray Castle, a lithograph by Moses Griffiths, 1760 (*Author's Collection*)

Inveraray Castle, 2003 (*Author's Collection*)

part of the building by an additional attic storey thereby improving the proportions in line with the criticism of Dr Johnson a century before. According to Boswell writing in his *Journal of a tour to the Hebrides* (1796): '[He] was much struck by the grandeur and elegance of this princely seat but thought the castle too low and wished it had been a storey higher.' Boswell's interests in the castle appeared to be otherwise engaged: 'I never shall forget the impression made upon my fancy by some of the ladies' maids tripping about in neat morning dresses . . . their lively manner and gay, inviting appearance pleased me so much that I thought for a moment I could have been a knight errant for them.'

One wonders how Dr Johnson might have viewed Salvin's further addition of tall slated cones on each of the four corner towers which give the castle a fairy-tale appearance.

Robert Mylne was responsible for the interior design of the castle. The lavish plaster ceilings, Gothic motifs in the north-east entrance hall and classical detail in the dining room and drawing room, were the work of John Clayton. Perhaps the best-known view of the castle, after its external elevation, is that of the extraordinary display of weaponry in the Armoury Hall. This is mainly the work of Robert Mylne with some twentieth-century additions.

The castle grounds also received great attention. A broad avenue of trees leads from the shore of the loch to the castle which is surrounded by formal gardens. Each of the entrances to the grounds is guarded by a lodge of distinct and varying design, either classical or rustic. There are a number of the follies so beloved by eighteenth-century architects, the most prominent of these being the watch tower high on the hill, overlooking Inverary town. In his bid to replace the runrig system of farming, the Duke introduced the rotation of crops in large-scale fields and built a number of farm complexes which included barn, stables, stores and offices. The largest of these steadings to have survived and in part to be restored is Maltland Square, situated near Carloonan.

Commemorating the Campbell Covenanting martyrs of the seventeenth century is a tall pillar capped by an urn. This stood in the square of the old town and was retained within the castle grounds following the reconstructions of the eighteenth century.

Following the accession of the 5th Duke, the work of rebuilding the town went on apace, requiring far more labour than the Duke could muster from among his own men. Irish and English workmen in their hundreds were brought in to perform the various skilled tasks

The Lands at Newtown, Inveraray (*Author's Collection*)

required. Temporary accommodation had to be found for them and trade flourished amongst the providers of services in the burgh.

Robert Mylne, who was the most prominent of the architects engaged by the 5th Duke, was responsible for the arches through which one must pass to reach the Dalmally road and for those fronting the magnificent avenue of beeches which leads to the nineteenth-century Episcopal All Saints Church, the separate Duke's Tower which was erected in 1923–31; its ten bells are inscribed in Latin with the names of Gaelic saints.

The three-storey tenement buildings, known as the Relief Land, framing the main street, are the work of Robert Mylne.

It was in one of these houses that poet, writer and historian, Neil Munro (1864–1930), was born. Munro, the illegitimate son of a serving maid, was raised in the tenement block called Crombie's Land. Neil's mother married Malcolm Thompson, the Governor of Inveraray Jail, when the boy was thirteen. Through the good offices of his stepfather, Neil became apprenticed to William Douglas, lawyer and Sheriff's Clerk to Argyll. At the age of eighteen he went to Glasgow, eventually becoming a full-time journalist with the Glasgow *Evening News* in 1884, by which time he had already had a number of articles and short stories published. In 1896 he published his first book of short stories and there followed a number of historical novels, one in particular, *The New Road* (1914), being considered his finest work. It was, however, his tales of Para Handy and the crew of the Clyde puffer, *The Vital Spark*, which brought Neil his greatest fame. Of his early beginnings he once wrote: 'The things we love intensely are the things worth writing about. I could never keep Inveraray out of any story of mine and I never will . . . this parish is a miniature of the world.' When he was well known as a writer, Neil returned most summers to Inveraray with his family, staying in the house which had formerly belonged to his first employer, William Douglas, the House of the Brass Man's Hand in Main Street. A memorial to Munro stands on a rise just above the town on the Dalmally road.

Materials for building the new town had to be brought in from the Duke's vast estates – stone from the quarries at Creggan, Crarae, and St Catherines, marble from Ardmaddy and Iona, lead from Strontian, slates from Easdale and timber from the Duke's own parklands. The Creggan quarry, only a few miles down the loch, yielded a chloritic schist which is soft like soapstone when freshly cut but which hardens in air to form a very hard stone with a polished surface, highly resistant to weathering. When wet, this stone is black in appearance but in bright sunlight is a curious bluish-grey colour. Pennant in his *Tour in Scotland* (1769) describes it as 'a coarse form of lapis ollaris, similar to a blue stone found in Norway from which the Royal palace at Copenhagen was constructed'.

While Inveraray had up to this date always been described as a 'town', an ancient prediction denied this. Legend has it that Niven MacVicar, the parson of Kilmalieu who had been a priest of Rome in the sixteenth century before he embraced Protestantism at the Reformation, possessed the gift of second sight. He predicted that Inveraray would never be a town until the bell rang on Creagan nan Caorach. This is a rocky headland projecting into the loch a little to the south of the burgh. People puzzled for long over the cleric's words until Glenaray and Inveraray Parish Church, designed by Robert Mylne, was erected in the town centre between 1792 and 1802 and the bell was hung in a circular opening in the south gable. It was then realised that the special stone required for the tower had been quarried from Creagan nan Caorach! The settlement could now legitimately call itself a town. The bell, which had been taken from the earlier parish church of Kilmalieu, bears the date 1728.

Parish Church of All Saints, Inveraray (*Author's Collection*)

Inveraray Parish Church is unusual in having been built partitioned in order to provide two churches, one for Gaelic worship and the other for English. Until the 1960s, services were regularly conducted in both languages but with the decline in the number of Gaelic speakers in the burgh, the Gaelic church fell into disrepair. In the late 1950s this part of the building underwent a face-lift and is now in regular use as the church hall.

After the Reformation, Niven MacVicar was known to be ambivalent about some aspects of the Reformed Church. Rather than antagonise one party or the other by using the same font to baptise both Protestant and Catholic babies, he is said to have hollowed out a second font at the base of the original, baptising those of the new Faith in the lower one and those of the old in the upper basin. In support of this story, the medieval font, transported to the new church, certainly bears a hollowed-out section at its base.

In 1640 in compliance with the ruling of the Privy Council to provide education for the first-born son of every gentleman in the parish, the Synod of Argyll agreed to set up a grammar school at

Inveraray. The school did not open until 1650 but when it did, it took in pupils from all over the Earl's territory in mid- and south Argyll. Because of the great distances involved many of the pupils were boarders.

The original grammar school was demolished along with other public buildings in the old town. A new grammar school was built along one side of the main square of the new town. The building was to undergo many changes before 1907 when the present façade was completed. By the terms of the new Education Act, in 1873 the school was obliged to take in every child in the parish between the ages of five and eleven years and, since it also provided secondary education for those who could afford it, considerable extensions and alterations were made. The grammar school never lost its title despite the fact that in 1944 its full secondary status was removed. In 1961 the grammar school had one hundred pupils on roll. Each of the larger townships on the Earl's estate and the one or two villages such as Furnace and Achnagoul in Glen Shira had their own primary schools but most of these had been closed by 2000 because they were no longer viable.

The prosperity engendered by all the building activity of the eighteenth and early nineteenth centuries could not last. By the first decade of the nineteenth century the building work had been largely completed and much of the additional labour departed. The town settled down to its regular routine and many of the inhabitants found it hard to make a living.

The 5th Duke's energies were now concentrated upon finding alternative forms of employment for his people. He initiated training in the spinning and weaving of linen, setting up a school in Inveraray to teach the women the skills of the trade. One complete floor of Factory Land (1774), the tenement on the shore, south of the jail, is a large spinning workroom. This initiative he repeated in various parts of his domains and for some time the county of Argyll was a major producer of linen goods. Quarries, opened up to provide materials for building Inveraray, now produced for a wider market, the stone being transported by sea to the cities of the south. Crarae quarry is said to have produced most of the paving setts for Glasgow's streets.

For centuries fishing has been one of the main forms of employment in the parish. Both Thomas Pennant and Dorothy Wordsworth in their accounts of their journeys through the Highlands, speak of the massed fleets of fishing vessels at the head of Loch Fyne. During the herring season the town would be overwhelmed by the influx of seamen and barrels of salted fish were piled up on the quay. Despite the 3rd Duchess's objections to the smell of fish, which had necessitated the building of Newtown to the south of the burgh, the new village was unable to cope with the influx of boats during those few weeks when the herring were running in the loch. At such times much of the activity reverted to the town quay.

It was the abundance of fish caught at this season, and the necessity of finding a way to preserve it satisfactorily, that encouraged the emergence of smokeries up and down the coast and the production of the now world-famous oak-smoked Loch Fyne kippers. With stocks of wild fish so sadly depleted along the western coasts, Loch Fyne has in the last twenty years become an important fish-farming location. The local salmon and trout farms now employ more people than the coastal and deep-sea fishing industry.

Soon after development of the new town began, it became clear that there was an urgent need for good-quality accommodation for a growing number of businessmen and tourists and priority was given to the construction of the planned Great Inn. Now the Argyll Arms Hotel, the inn was completed in 1755. At the time it was acclaimed as being the finest inn in Scotland. The landlord had come from England bringing with him the latest ideas about the operation of a hotel and installing the most up-to-date conveniences. What he provided was the utmost luxury for those wishing to explore the wild Highlands the easy way!

As a first venture in tourism the Great Inn was highly successful. When the journals of those early travellers were published, their accounts created wide interest and very soon more and more people were coming via Inveraray to visit the Highlands.

Soon after her accession, Queen Victoria began her regular visits to Scotland. She made no secret of her enthusiasm for all things Scottish and for the followers of royal fashion a Highland holiday became a must, preferably in one's own private retreat. Not only did the 8th Duke of Argyll make money from the sale of small parcels of land to the newly rich industrialists but, like his Breadalbane cousins, he invested in the tourism industry in a big way. More hotels were built, public transport in the form of horse-drawn buses was introduced and round trips were devised in conjunction with certain Glasgow transport companies.

With the introduction of powerful steam-propelled shipping, early in the nineteenth century, regular passenger travel by sea became a possibility. The first steamers to ply Loch Fyne were owned by David Napier, who, in 1826, launched a regular steamer service between Inveraray and St Catherines and also introduced pleasure trips around the loch. In 1836 the Lochgoil and Loch Long Steamer Company, which was already carrying Glaswegians to Lochgoilhead and Castle Carrick, acquired the Loch Fyne ferry rights using a small paddle steamer described by one disgruntled rival as a 'washtub of a steamer'. It was no unfair criticism, however, for the ship took an hour to complete the two-mile crossing from Inveraray to St Catherines.

The pier at Inveraray was enlarged to take the Clyde pleasure steamers and regular excursions were arranged. One might travel from Glasgow by water, disembark at Inveraray and take a horse-drawn bus to Dalmally. There the trippers joined the railway to complete the round trip to Glasgow. Alternatively, passengers might disembark at Lochgoilhead and take a drive over the Rest and Be Thankful to Inveraray, visit the castle grounds and return by steamer to Broomielaw Quay in Glasgow.

Apart from Inverary itself which, although small, has for long been considered a town, there are few settlements in the parish of Glenaray and Inveraray which can be described as anything more than a township. The few villages there date in the main from the late eighteenth century, their development owing much to the enterprise of the Duke. They are, however, usually sited on much older, but smaller, settlements. The parish might be viewed as one huge estate divided up into a series of farms under the direct control of the Duke. Only one true crofting village can be identified from the Ordnance Survey maps of the district – that at Auchindrain, a few miles south of Inverarary. Here, despite attempts by Archibald, the 5th Duke, to persuade the villagers to give up their runrigs and adopt his more modern methods of farming, the people retained the crofting system of management until economic necessity drove its occupants to move out in the middle of the twentieth century. Many of the cottages, some more than two hundred years old, had already fallen into decay when the last crofting family of MacCallums gave up the tenancy in 1962. This former village is a time capsule which, since being taken over by a charitable trust in 1964, has been lovingly restored as Auchindrain Township Open-air Museum.

Concerned for the well-being of all his people and determined to exploit the resources of his estates to the full, the 5th Duke extended his entrepreneurial activities throughout the parish.

MacCallum's House, *c.* 1800, Auchindrain Township Open-air Museum (*Author's Collection*)

The extensive woodlands provided fuel for the smelting of iron ore which could be imported cheaply by sea, the pig iron produced being sold to industries in the Clyde valley and northern England. For this purpose the Craleckan Ironworks was established at the small settlement of Inverleckan, a few miles down the loch. This was very soon to become known as Furnace.

The iron foundry was run by a firm of smelters from Ulverstone in Lancashire who, in 1753, made a survey of the Duke's woodlands and entered into lengthy negotiations to set up a furnace on the lochside. Charcoal for the smelters was burnt in the immediate vicinity giving employment to some local people. To accommodate the men and their families brought in to work the smelter, a village of workmen's cottages was built around the plant. A row of these foundry workers' cottages stands alongside the A83 Lochgilphead to Inveraray road which today bypasses the main part of the village. A landing stage was built to accommodate the transport vessels and it was thought necessary to provide an inn for the comfort of visiting businessmen and the entertainment of foundry workers and seamen. The inn still provides food and accommodation for travellers as well as acting as a focal point of village life.

Iron furnace, Furnace (formerly Inverleckan) (*Author's Collection*)

When iron smelting ceased in 1812, charcoal production continued and some years later the Furnace works turned its attention to the manufacture of gunpowder. Saltpetre and sulphur, the other ingredients, were imported from South America and the production of explosives continued for fifty years. Unfortunately, houses built in close proximity to an iron foundry proved to be very vulnerable with a powder works for a neighbour! The operation ceased in 1883 when a severe explosion killed the works manager and destroyed much of the plant; miraculously, neither the nearby school nor the post office was destroyed.

Without alternative employment the village quickly emptied, its inhabitants moving to the cities to find work. Today improved transport offers access to alternative forms of employment and a very viable and active community resides there.

The quarry at Crarae, opened up in order to provide stone for the building of the castle, continued in operation well into the nineteenth century and once steamer excursions from Glasgow began, the sight of a quarry at work proved to be a tremendous attraction for visitors. After a while, quarry blasting was being timed to coincide with the arrival of the steamer from Glasgow. Passengers crowded the deck to witness the spectacle of great quantities of rock flying from the face of the cliff to tumble to the ground below.

By 1883 the thirst for industrial explosions had become so intense that a party consisting of the Lord Provost of Glasgow and the Provosts of Govan and Kenning Park watched a spectacular blast at the iron foundry at Furnace from the deck of *Lord of the Isles*. Three years later, a thousand holidaymakers witnessed an even bigger blast at Crarae. Following this explosion, some of the excursionists actually jumped overboard and swam ashore while a dense cloud of fine dust particles hung above the quarry. A dog and then a child became asphyxiated and were carried from the scene. Soon six adults had died of asphyxia or were poisoned by the sulphurous fumes. The breathing of twenty more was seriously affected. From then on the steamer company steered clear of blasting operations.

At the time of greatest activity in the Crarae quarries the nearby village of Minard, hitherto little more than a township, began to expand in order to provide accommodation and services for quarry workers. Little is known of the early history of this village. The ancient churchyard of Killevin suggests a priest's cell and a medieval church on this spot. The most prominent memorial is a rubble wall with corniced coping stone surrounding a rectangular burial plot, dating from 1727. This is the Campbell enclosure where members of a local branch of the clan are buried. Two small churches in use today are the Lochfyneside Free Church, a simple rectangular construction with a large bell-cote and paired, pointed arch windows and Lochfyneside Church, a prefabricated corrugated-iron building erected in 1910, having an octagonal stained-glass oriel window in the gable-end.

Fire damage to the castle at Inveraray in 1877 brought about further activity in the quarries as stone was hewn for the additional storey which was built at that time. By the early nineteenth century Minard had its own village shop and school. The post office building and adjacent houses date from the mid-nineteenth century.

The village may attribute its later development to the presence of Minard Castle, originally built as a modest family home in 1775. Much altered in the mid-nineteenth century, it is now a pretentious Victorian mansion with corbelled and crenellated parapets and an elaborately Gothic interior. Without doubt the development of this grand house brought much-needed employment to those villagers engaged as servants or estate workers.

In the 1950s the Forestry Commission built a row of workers

cottages in the centre of the village, a short distance back from the road. The village population was almost doubled overnight and although Forest Enterprise is no longer such a large employer of labour, the presence of these additional houses, which were sold off privately some years ago, has ensured a steady flow of new blood into the area. With the regionalisation of Scotland in 1976, Strathclyde set up a new administrative centre at Kilmory, a little to the north in the parish of Kilmichael Glassary. An influx of local government officers placed additional demands upon available housing stocks.

Between the quarry and the village of Minard, the Crarae burn cuts its way down through a deep gorge to join Loch Fyne. In 1925 the Cumlodden estate, through which the burn flows, was purchased by Captain, later Sir George Campbell, a gentleman who had spent some considerable part of his life in India. Reminded of his experiences abroad, Sir George decided to create a Himalayan ravine out of the magnificent gorge down which the Crarae burn plunges in spectacular waterfalls. He imported azaleas and rhododendrons together with other exotic species from all around the world. The steep-sided gorge was planted with noble conifers while on the lower levels clumps of tropical bamboo intermingle with eucalyptus from Australia. The gardens provide employment as gardeners, guides, and caterers for the many visitors they attract.

The parish and burgh of Glenaray and Inveraray have seen little change since the completion of the new town two hundred years ago. The parish church dominates the top of the High Street and the road which crosses it at right angles is still paved in cobble setts. The Courthouse and jail remain unaltered, a monument to the days when the Campbells were all-powerful. The fine buildings set around the square house shops as well as domestic dwellings and between the main street and the harbour wall a number of restaurants and hotels provide for the needs of the visitors who flock into the town in the summer season.

The population of the parish fell from 2,285 in 1871 to 990 in 1931. The Second World War saw an influx of military personnel when not only British but Polish, and latterly, United States soldiers were encamped in four locations: two camps were situated behind the Lands to the south of the town on the Lochgilphead road, one was in the castle grounds and the fourth in Glen Shira. For a few years the loch was again crowded with vessels of all kinds, in particular landing craft used in training for the expected invasion of Europe.

In the post-war years major hydroelectric developments at Cruachan and in Glen Shira kept up the numbers resident in the burgh but thereafter there was a steady decline until in 1980 a figure of 500 was recorded. Numbers stayed fairly static in the last years of the twentieth century, the restrictions upon land used for building and conservation of the historic town preventing any but the most modest housing developments. Usually the only new construction allowed to take place is upon the foundations of a previous building or to meet the immediate needs of the existing population. To this end three blocks of tenements, housing twelve families, were built in 1938 to the south of the town, while in the early 1960s the Local Authority provided further dwellings to compensate for the loss of houses in the main square which had been demolished to make way for a garage. Inveraray lost its County Burgh status after Argyll became part of Strathclyde Region in 1975.

Communications have been very much improved in the last fifty years but until these improvements were completed, heavy goods and materials were still being brought in by sea, although the main steamer passenger lines ceased their operation before the Second World War. The vessels used for carrying cargo were the puffers celebrated in Neil Munro's Para Handy stories. The *Eilean Eisdeal*, the last working puffer operating on the west coast, who spent her final

Puffer *Eilean Eisdale* at Easdale, *c.* 1990 (*Author's Collection*)

working days until the late 1990s based at Easdale, has recently been restored and converted for carrying a small number of passengers. She is currently moored at Inverary Pier.

One cannot complete an account of the burgh and parish of Glenaray and Inveraray without reference to the uniquely Celtic game of shinty. Believed to have been the home of the game, Inveraray can certainly boast its oldest ever player for Provost William Brown played on his hundredth birthday! This gentleman's table-top grave in Kilmalieu graveyard records that he lived from 1603 to 1711. The Minute Book of Inveraray's team, known as the Yellow and Black, records that on 12 January 1877 members met in the armoury of the Volunteers. Twenty members were present including four from the township of Achnagoul. Today the shinty stick, or caman, costs in excess of £10 but in 1879 the club engaged a local man to make them at a cost of two shillings each. Sticks are made from ash or oak branches grown to the required shape. At first a wooden ball was used which, together with the wild swinging of the sticks to heads and ankles, made the game a pretty dangerous affair. Travel to matches must have presented a considerable challenge to the team in the early days, often necessitating a very long walk before the game! By 1870 shinty had become a national game played from Glasgow northwards throughout the Highlands. Requiring no regular boundaries and not needing a particularly flat ground, it was the ideal sport for this region. Inveraray's shinty team continues to flourish. The oldest trophy, the Challenge Cup, has been won at least ten times by the Yellow and Black and the Camanachd or Scottish Cup at least six times.

3
CRAIGNISH AND KILMELFORD

Sea lochs and scenery, gunpowder, fish farming and marinas

A Scottish relative once remarked to me, when I expressed a desire to live on the coast of Argyll, that it was all very well on a fine summer's day, 'but you can't live on scenery'. This was in the 1950s when the Clyde shipyards were still busy, General Motors were churning out Hilman cars in their thousands at Johnstone and the coal mines and steelworks of Lanarkshire were in full production. Any suggestion that tourism was going to be Scotland's major industry of the future would have been greeted with mirth and derision in the bars and tearooms of Sauchiehaul and Princes Streets. Fifty years on, Argyll is in the forefront of the development of time-share apartments and holiday complexes, hotels, B&Bs and caravan parks, providing every facility and luxury for visitors. At the beginning of the third millennium, in the parishes of Craignish and neighbouring Kilmelford and Kilninver, tourism is the mainstay of many of the older villages and has resulted in the creation of at least one new one.

Neolithic man set up his first settlements in Craignish on the islands which crowd into the head of this long, narrow sea loch. The Picts occupied caves along the peninsula and marked their presence by monoliths, cists, cairns, and crannogs. A single standing stone holds a commanding position on a hillock at the head of the loch.

By the time the Craignish peninsula was visited by Christian missionaries from Ireland in the middle of the sixth century, there was a substantial population to be converted to the Christian faith. In the centuries that followed, this valuable, fertile area was coveted by many invaders from the outer islands and from northern Europe. To counter such attacks, a number of hill forts were constructed at strategic points.

The first Christian settlement, named after the Virgin Mary, Kilmarie, was almost certainly at the village of Kirkton halfway along the south-eastern shore of the peninsula. On this same site there are substantial ruins of a medieval church. The burial ground, which is still in use, contains Early Christian burial slabs with incised crosses and several fourteenth- and fifteenth-century tapered slabs. Kilmarie was the old parish church of Craignish and served Craignish Castle, situated a mile or so to the north, overlooking Loch Beag.

The first reference to a castle at Craignish in the estate records is 1414 when substantial repairs were carried out. The building may possibly date back to the twelfth or thirteenth century and probably replaced an earlier earthwork on the same site, built as a defence against the Viking invaders. Constructed by the Campbells of Craignish, the present castle holds an impregnable position overlooking the Sound of Jura, its seaward approaches guarded by the famous Corrievreckan whirlpool. It was a bold invader who attempted to take his galleys through those raging waters and into the strong tidal rip of Dorus Mor, Big Door, at the entrance to the loch.

To the Vikings, Loch Craignish would have presented a great temptation. Its islands offered protected anchorage and the surrounding lands, ample supplies of food and fresh water. Many fierce battles ensued between the Scots and their Norse invaders. Witness to this are innumerable cairns where the dead of many a gruesome skirmish lie buried. The bulk of these are situated in one particular spot however, beside Baigh Dal nan Ceann, 'Bay of the Field of Heads'. Whatever the outcome of individual battles in the medieval period, the castle remained in the hands of the Campbells of Craignish and withstood all attempts to unseat the incumbents for the next five centuries.

Late in the seventeenth century, during the conflict led by the Marquess of Montrose in which a band of Scottish Royalists attempted to restore the Crown of the United Kingdom to the deposed King James II, Craignish Castle came under siege by a band of Irish mercenaries under the command of Colla Ciotach Macdonald (the left-handed Coll). Their plan was to seize the rather less-defended Duntroon Castle, on the opposite shore of the loch, and then to attack Craignish. The Campbell laird, being informed of the plan, laid an ambush for the attackers by substantially increasing the garrison holding Duntroon.

It seems that in an earlier conflict, Colla's favourite piper had been captured and imprisoned in Duntroon Castle. Now, as the Macdonald's birlinns (galleys) approached the entrance to the loch, the imprisoned piper played a particular piobaireachd to warn his master that the Campbells had set a trap for him. Steering his galleys away just in time, Macdonald was saved to fight another day. The unfortunate piper however, was slain for his part in the affair!

It was left to Colla's son to seek revenge for his father's humiliation. Some years later, Alexander Macdonald returned, this time to attack Craignish Castle, directly. He had been heard to describe the stronghold disparagingly as 'that little castle of welks! A puff of wind will make it tremble.' He soon discovered his mistake. Having found the castle so heavily defended as to be impregnable, in a few weeks he gave up and went away.

In 1691 the Craignish estate was one of the Campbell holdings to be confiscated as punishment for the rebellious 7th Earl. It came under the control of the Earl of Atholl who had been instructed to lay waste all Argyll's property and to kill off his henchmen.

The captain of Craignish Castle cleared his barns of anything of value and removed the womenfolk and children together with all his livestock, to the islands in the loch. He then returned to the mainland with a band of warriors and waylaid Atholl's men. The invaders were completely overwhelmed at a little bay which was forever after called Port nan Athullach (Athollmen's port). Atholl never returned to the place of his humiliation and with the general pardon issued by King William, the Campbells could legitimately reassume their captaincy of Craignish.

When the estate was finally broken up in 1860 the castle, together with the south-western end of the peninsula, came into the hands of a Yorkshire family, the Gascoines. In 1954 the castle and its policies were purchased by a Mr McEwan, later Lord Younger, of the Scottish brewing family. Lord Younger had the building divided into four apartments which were each sold off separately providing distinguished holiday accommodation for their owners.

Situated on the Craignish peninsula is the village of Ardfern. Early references to this village are sparse and there is little doubt that until the seventeenth century, regular communication with other parts of the county being by sea, most of the business of the parish was conducted at Kirktoun. With the development of an improved road system, however, Ardfern became the centre of the parish.

There is record of a school for labourers' children having been provided as early as 1698 but the present Ardfern school was built by the Gascoines in 1861. In 1951 it was described as a small building divided by a removable partition in which twenty-five children of all ages were taught. At that time the building was said to be poorly

Marina at Ardfern (*Author's Collection*)

ventilated and lit only by a few small windows set high in the walls. It was not until 2001 that the original building was substantially altered and extended to bring it up to modern-day requirements.

The present parish church at Ardfern was built in 1826 on the site of two earlier buildings dated 1698 and 1730 respectively. The church had fallen into such poor condition that in his 1951 statistical account, the Rev. Neil Mackay feared it might have to be abandoned. Clearly the parishioners considered it worth saving for with financial support from the heritors, repairs were eventually put in hand to repair it.

Today the village boasts a splendid new village hall replacing its 1930s concrete and corrugated-iron predecessor and to accommodate a growing fleet of pleasure craft of all kinds, a new pier and marina were constructed during the last quarter of the twentieth century.

Until the 1930s, the parish existed on a self-sufficient basis. Steamers plied the coastal route transporting both passengers and goods to and from Glasgow but imported goods were expensive. Most people depended upon themselves and their neighbours for the necessities of life. According to the statistical accounts of 1841 and 1861, in the village of Ardfern could be found weavers, millers operating flax and corn mills, a blacksmith, a tailor, a bootmaker and every kind of support for village life. Today many people are self-employed, often engaged in the provision of facilities for the tourism industry. This may take the form of the production of arts and crafts for sale or the provision of accommodation and other services. The numbers of those now employed on the land are much reduced from former times. Although fishing is no longer a significant industry here, a limited number of people are employed by the fish farms set up during the 1980s and 1990s.

In 1724, the population of the parish was over 1,000 and in the 1841 statistical account, a figure of 873 was recorded. By 1901, however, following a major alteration in the parish boundaries, the population had fallen to 327. Many factors combined to bring about this decline. The amalgamation of a number of smaller farms into two huge ones substantially reduced the farming population and there was a steady exodus from the parish. By 1951 the number had fallen to around 200. Any further drain on the indigenous population was arrested when, in the late 1950s, a number of Local Authority houses were erected at Ardfern. In the 1980s, however, these homes were offered for purchase by their sitting tenants and now form a part of the privately owned housing stock. With the increased demand for retirement and second homes, house prices are rising and the shortage of affordable housing for local young people is once again driving them away to the lowlands in search of work and cheaper homes.

The agricultural land of the peninsula, once divided into a large number of small crofts, was amalgamated into a small number of large farms at the beginning of the nineteenth century. These farms were associated with the larger houses in the parish, Barbreck, Lunga and Stonefield Castle. Each of these supported its own community of workers providing accommodation in small townships. Substantial steadings for housing animals and storing crops were also created. The farms supported the great houses and provided the local community with fresh produce of every kind. In the late nineteenth century the largest farms were again split into smaller units but towards the end of the twentieth century, they were once more amalgamated into three large farms of which two concentrate upon rearing stock for the meat market. The third has overcome the exigencies of a maritime climate by resorting to the use of poly-tunnels in order to raise vegetables and fruit to meet the growing demand for fresh, organically grown produce.

The northern section of the parish is mainly agricultural land occupying the valley of the Barbreck River where it drains into the headwaters of Loch Craignish. Standing in a dominant position overlooking the loch is Barbreck House. The Barbreck estate was owned by the Campbells of Barbreck from as early as the fifteenth century but in 1732 the lands were forfeited and control passed to the 4th Duke of Argyll in 1768. The Duke appointed his kinsman, Sir John Campbell, a distinguished soldier descended from the Campbells of Lochnell, to be his tacksman.

The present Barbreck House, situated on rising ground at the head of the loch, was built by Sir John in 1790. It is an imposing residence with classically simple elevations and elegant proportions. The house is of three storeys and is five bays in width. The three central bays bear a classical pediment capped by an urn. Single-storey wings are linked to right and left by arcaded walls and the eaves cornices are also decorated with urns. At the rear the two wings are extended to provide service areas, a laundry, stables and a byre and are joined behind the house to form a U-shaped courtyard. The grounds contain a folly, popular in important buildings of the late eighteenth century, and a family mausoleum with pyramid roof.

The farms associated with Barbreck House were sold off separately during the nineteenth century so that by the 1950s statistical account, eight farms were recorded. Towards the end of the twentieth century, however, these were again amalgamated to form one large Barbreck Farm. The township of Barbreck has its own burial ground whose earliest gravestone is dated 1814. The presence of a separate graveyard for the estate suggests a large population here in Victorian times. It

Traditional hayricks (*Author's Collection*)

seems that prior to the 1790s all burials in the parish took place at Kilmarie Church.

Much of the higher ground on the peninsula has poor soil with rocky outcrops making stock-raising the only truly viable kind of farming. In the Barbreck valley, however, grain crops can be grown and for many centuries the local bere or barley has supplied the distilleries in the area. Other crops produced until the mid-twentieth century were oats, turnips, potatoes and forage crops to see the cattle through the winter months. With the exception of a small herd of dairy cows providing milk to the local population, the cattle are reared for the meat market. Silage, contained in ugly black silage bags, provide the winter feed of the twenty-first century. Sadly, those neatly stacked, rum-baba-shaped hayricks, which I remember from my childhood and which were once unique to the Scottish landscape, are now a thing of the past.

Outwith the modern village of Craobh Haven, on the northern shore of the peninsula, stands Lunga House. Originally, a sixteenth-century tower house built by the Campbells stood on the site but this was almost totally destroyed in reconstruction work which took place during the seventeenth century. In 1785, the property and surrounding lands were conveyed to John MacDougall of Lunga who also made substantial alterations. The result is a conglomeration of styles, part battlemented, part baronial and some Gothic. Greatly altered and restored to modern-day standards, the house is now run as a hotel while estate cottages and converted farm steadings are let as self-catering accommodation. Close by, steadings of the original house have been converted to a substantial riding stables and riding school.

Lunga House remains in MacDougall hands to this day, although much of the estate land was sold off for the development of the late twentieth-century model village of Craobh Haven. MacDougall sons who died in two world wars are commemorated by a fine cross which stands at the head of the main street of the new village.

Designed as a holiday centre with shops, chandlery and marina, the village of Craobh Haven was established in 1983. This was one enterprising company's solution to the problem of accommodating growing numbers of holidaymakers, the demand being for self-catering facilities of a standard many of the traditional houses in the locality were unable to provide. The new houses are, in the main, privately owned and occupied as holiday homes, others are let out

MacDougall stone, Kilmarie Churchyard (*Author's Collection*)

by the week. Some are permanent homes. The sheltered marina, constructed by linking two small islands with a breakwater, attracts enthusiasts for yachting and other water sports. The houses represent a variety of Scottish styles of architecture. Round stair towers and slated pinnacles recall the fairy-tale silhouette of Inveraray Castle while tall narrow town houses are reminiscent of eighteenth-century Oban. Traditional harling is coloured in the pastel shades of a Spanish town while at the centre is a green suggesting village cricket and muffins for tea! Although variously described by critics as sentimental, romantic or quaint, Craobh Haven fulfils its purpose admirably and is steadily taking on the mantle of a permanent settlement, occupied for twelve months of the year. In its struggle to become recognised by the Local Authority as a legitimate beneficiary of such services as decent road access, traffic calming and street lighting, the village community has come together as a force to be reckoned with. Craobh Haven is an excellent example of the way in which holiday provision can be introduced into the Highlands without detriment to the existing environment.

Much of the parish of Kilmelford and Kilninver, particularly that part lying to the west of the A816, is an area of pre-Cambrian rocks sandwiched between intrusions of hard dolerite and andesitic material emanating from the Tertiary volcanic complex on the island of Mull. The resulting topography is one of hilly crags, steep-sided gullies and long narrow glens formed by the erosion of the older schistose rocks. The land is of little agricultural value and was once heavily wooded. It would have been a haunt of wild animals and with the mountain streams and lochans teeming with fish the area was certainly attractive to the hunter-gatherers of prehistoric times. There is abundant evidence of this in the numerous Iron Age forts and duns of the region. Blasting operations carried out by Scottish Hydro Board in 1956 above the village of Melfort exposed a cave of great archaeological significance. Several hundred flint and bone artefacts were uncovered as well as teeth and charcoal fragments dating from 5000 BC. Bronze Age artefacts, now in the National Museums of Scotland, which were found during excavations for the foundations for the present Melfort House included two beautifully worked metal armlets and a crescent-shaped necklace of jet beads. A crannog, just offshore, is thought to be of medieval age.

Castles or fortified houses existed at Arduaine, Melfort, Ardanstur, Kilchoan, Degnish and Ardmaddy and all were at one time or another in the hands of the Clan Campbell. It was the MacDougalls, the Lords of Lorn, however, who first laid claim to these lands, building their stronghold, a hill fort, at Raera or Reray on a hill overlooking the mouth of Loch Feochan above the valley of the River Euchar and the present-day village of Kilninver. During the thirteenth century the MacDougalls moved their headquarters down to the shores of Balvicar Bay and built a new fortified dwelling at Ardmaddy.

In 1343 King David granted all the forfeited MacDougall lands to Gilleasbuig Mor (Great Archibald) Campbell, Knight of Lochow and the parish of Melfort and Kilninver came into the hands of his half-brother Neil Campbell who founded the family branch, the Campbells of Melfort. Neil reconstructed Ardmaddy and lived there but later members of the family built at Melfort. The Campbell succession of ownership was unbroken until 1838 when a large part of the Melfort estate was sold to a company manufacturing gunpowder. During a period of more than a hundred years from the late eighteenth until the turn of the twentieth century, from the Napoleonic to the South African wars, the Campbells of Melfort contributed an extraordinary number of servicemen to the armed forces. They can boast two Admirals, one Captain RN, one Commander RN, four Generals, four Colonels, two Majors, six Captains and six Lieutenants. Three of them were Knights Commander of the Bath, two were Governors of British Colonies and one was Governor of Fort George. Many of the men died on active service.

Nor was the contribution of this great estate to Britain's naval and military power restricted to its fighting men. In the eighteenth century the practice of charcoal burning was introduced to the ancient oak woods of the Melfort estate as an adjunct to the manufacture of gunpowder. Harrison Ainsley & Co., an English armaments manufacturing company, purchased part of the Melfort estate in 1838 with the express intention of making gunpowder. The site was ideal for the purpose. The vital ingredients, sulphur and saltpetre, had to be imported from South America and the village of Melfort offered a substantial pier and a safe anchorage for the cargo vessels from abroad. The River Oude which flowed through the site was capable of being dammed to control a flow of water to the mills while the surrounding woodlands, properly managed, would provide charcoal sufficient for all their needs. The site was a reasonable distance from human habitation and protected at the rear by steep cliffs which would contain any explosion. An extended Melfort village provided suitable accommodation for the workers at the powder mill.

The traditional method of burning charcoal was to stack the wood in heaps for burning and cover it with turf or peats to exclude oxygen. Under these conditions the wood burned to charcoal rather than ash. Charcoal made in this manner was perfectly satisfactory for the smelting of iron but was insufficiently pure for incorporation in black powder for blasting. At Melfort a new system of distilling the burning wood in sealed retorts resulted in a much more uniform product. Each of the ingredients had to be pulverised and sifted a number of times, separately, before the ingredients could be blended together. At this stage there was always danger of explosion and there were a number of small incidents with damage to buildings and injury to workers. In 1867, however, there was a major explosion resulting in the destruction of several of the buildings and a number of severe injuries. Repairs were made and work resumed for a while but by the end of the nineteenth century, black powder had been replaced by dynamite in the stone quarries and improvements to weaponry had eliminated the use of gunpowder. The Melfort works closed down.

The original Melfort House has long since disappeared although a court of offices built early in the nineteenth century, once incorporated in the powder works, now forms a part of the Melfort Holiday Village. Otherwise, only the walled garden remains. A new Melfort House was built near the site of the original in 1962 to a design by Leslie Grahame MacDougal. A strange admixture of South African-Dutch, hip and flat roofs, with a balconied and bowed front elevation, the mansion seems somewhat inappropriate amid the wooded slopes of the Degnish peninsular.

The Melfort estate was sold for agricultural purposes in 1871 and the buildings relating to the powder works were utilised for storage and as cattle byres. Fortunately, 120 years after the explosion which heralded the closure of the works, this large complex of eighteenth-century buildings has been carefully converted into a holiday complex. In meeting the requirements of an increasingly demanding tourism industry, the developers have managed to preserve the unique heritage of the old gunpowder works while creating from them outstanding accommodation in a delightful setting.

The Melfort Club opened its doors in the late 1980s and has acted as the trigger for further developments. Melfort village now has a fine pier, a large anchorage for pleasure craft of all kinds, a chandlery, village shop and further self-catering accommodation, all clustered around the harbour.

The village of Kilmelford is the largest settlement in this widespread parish. It appears to owe its main development as a village to the building of a road linking Oban with Campbeltown towards the end of the eighteenth century. Prior to this, the village stood on the road linking Loch Awe and Loch Avich with Loch Melfort, one of the routes which was taken by cattle drovers from the seventeenth century.

One of the earliest buildings in the village is Cuilfail Hotel, an eighteenth-century coaching inn which, in the nineteenth century, became a favoured venue for Victorian gentlemen anglers. At one time, some ten gillies were kept permanently on the staff of the hotel

Melfort holiday village (*Author's Collection*)

in order to provide visitors with guides to the prolific streams and lochans where game fish were to be had.

Eighteenth- and nineteenth-century houses of the original village straddle the steep, narrow road which winds over the hills to Loch Avich. Others cluster around the parish church, while those built closer to the present main road, prevent any widening and reduce the flow of modern-day traffic to acceptable speeds. Sadly, the widening that has of necessity taken place has incurred the removal of the rock gardens for which the Cuilfail Hotel was once renowned.

Today Kilmelford village boasts the only post office in the parish. It has survived, largely because of a substantial increase in population in the late twentieth century. A new housing development on the southern outskirts of the village has ensured a viable population for the first years of the new millennium. Unfortunately, this collection of rather unimaginative bungalows, standing upon a featureless plain, does little to enhance the village. It is a sad reflection upon both the developers and the Local Planning Authority that no effort was made to blend this very necessary housing stock with the more pleasing, older part of the village.

The present parish church of Kilmelford dates from the end of the nineteenth century. Standing out proudly against the hillside above

Culfail Hotel, Kilmelford (*Author's Collection*)

the main road, it is believed to have been built upon the foundations of the medieval church of St Maelrubha which would have been the parish church also serving Melfort village.

The old village school, dated 1876, stands on a steep hillside to the north of the village. It was closed in the 1980s and the village children now travel by school bus to Kilninver, ten miles down the road. The old school has become a private dwelling house.

It was not until 1823 that a public road was constructed to carry horse-drawn vehicles through the Pass of Melfort, northwards to the other main village of the parish, Kilninver. At that time the road ran along the bottom of a deeply cut gorge alongside the River Oude. Cataracts and waterfalls had gouged out this deep gully and the passage must have been a spectacular sight. It soon became apparent, however, that those passing through the gorge were in danger of falling rocks and late in the nineteenth century the decision was taken to cut a new roadway at a higher level. Early in the twentieth century, the dam, originally built by the gunpowder manufacturers to control the waters of the River Oude, was reinforced in order to supply the village of Melfort with water. Except in the wettest conditions when the barrier is lifted to prevent overflowing of the reservoir, the river valley through the pass is now dry.

Kilninver village, 2003 (*Author's Collection*)

The village of Kilninver stands on the banks of the River Euchar, on the southern shores of Loch Feochan. It has a long history dating from the time when the early Scottish kings were brought this way for burial on Iona. A Christian cell was established here in the sixth century and a natural, flat rock on the loch shore, the King's Stone, was used as a quay from which the royal remains could be carried aboard ship.

To the south of the village on the west bank of the Euchar is the oldest building in the village, Rarey House. The present house stands on the site of the original MacDougall stronghold, a fortified earthworks which was vacated in the late fifteenth century, for the family's new seat at Ardmaddy.

Rarey or Raera House was built in 1743 as the tacksman's residence for the Campbell landlord of the day. Originally a single-storey building it was subsequently extended to provide a second storey and additional wing which accounts for its present L-shaped profile.

Over the years, Kilninver village developed at the junction of the main public road from Oban with the steep narrow track which ran over Kilninver Brae to Ardmaddy Castle, Balvicar and Easdale. The village street was a winding lane which climbed from the church in the Euchar valley up a steep hill to the schoolhouse which now stands on the new main road. The church, built in 1891 on the site of an earlier church dated 1792, is a small rectangular building perched on a knoll a little above the road. The original burial ground for the village lies on a second knoll high above the church, its Early Christian and medieval monuments indicating the great age of the village. A more recent burial plot, surrounded by a high stone wall, is sited alongside the old road close to the shore.

Early in the nineteenth century the village held the distinction of housing the first post office to serve the Slate Islands. This was an important role at a time when the slate quarries were at their peak of productivity and the population of the parish of Kilbrandon and Kilchattan was in excess of 2,000 people. A runner brought post daily from collecting points as far away as Ardmaddy, Easdale and Balvicar delivering letters to Kilninver for franking. Post was then carried on horseback to Oban and thence to Inverness, Glasgow or Edinburgh. By the end of the nineteenth century the post was sent by sea from Blackmill Bay on the Isle of Luing but Kilninver post office continued in use until the last quarter of the twentieth century. The original post office was housed in a tiny whitewashed cottage but was later transferred to the two-storey house next door, built in the early 1900s. Although the Kilninver post office has long been closed, there is still one of the old red telephone boxes standing outside the cottage to remind us of former days.

The present school and master's house were built in the 1870s. Today a small development of houses built in the 1950s forms a nucleus of a village beside the school building but there is neither shop nor village hall to create a focus for village life. The school is charged with this responsibility, its premises being used for innumerable social functions outside school hours.

In the 1970s the decision was made to upgrade the A816 by widening and straightening some of the worst sections. The new road bypasses the lower village including the church and the old post office and takes a higher course away from the river. The old and new approaches to the upper village join a few yards short of the school.

Much of the remainder of the parish is in the charge of the Forestry Commission and such habitation as there is consists of scattered farms. At the head of Loch Scammadale to the east of Kilmelford is the small township of Scammadale which comprises a number of cottages and houses whose occupants are mainly engaged in work on the surrounding agricultural land. This is one of the few townships

Pleasure craft on Loch Melfort, 1900 (*Easdale Museum*)

still in single ownership, the cottages being leased to their tenants by the heritors.

This end of the parish offers little employment. Agriculture is conducted on a family basis with the odd farmworker helping out. Forestry is the major function of the landscape but today mechanisation has reduced those employed to just a handful of men.

To the north of Craobh Haven at the head of Loch Melfort is the village of Arduaine, a small scattering of cottages spread across a steep hillside which descends to a narrow coastal strip hardly wide enough to carry the main road from Lochgilphead to Oban. Here is sited one of the oldest and largest fish-farming enterprises in Argyll. With sea fishing on the decline, the appearance of fish farms in many of Scotland's sea lochs has provided alternative employment for some redundant fishermen. The introduction of fish farming to the region has had a mixed reception from the locals over the past twenty-five years. While it is true that the supermarket shelves can be filled relatively cheaply by their produce, these unsightly developments detract from the natural beauty of the waters and also appear to have a deleterious effect upon the environment and in particular upon the wild fish stocks – a serious consideration in an area which depends greatly upon income from sporting anglers, fishing lochs and streams which were once renowned for their copious stocks of game fish.

A little to the north of the village a stubby finger of higher ground juts out into Loch Melfort separating it from the sheltered waters of Asknish Bay. It was here that in 1897, Arthur Campbell, a much-travelled gentleman with a passion for gardening, settled down to begin work upon his own unique legacy to the nation.

The windswept western coasts of Argyll are, at first sight, the last place any sensible gardener would choose to plant rare and exotic species, but that is precisely what Campbell decided to do. With the Gulf Stream flowing only yards offshore, providing a micro-climate with year-round temperatures which would support semi-tropical plants, he realised that, provided he could avoid the searing, salt-laden winds, he might plant a garden to remind him of all those exotic places he had visited. Using indigenous species which he supposed would have the best chance of survival, within a few years he had not only a substantial windbreak but gardens laid out much as we see them today. Like so many of his contemporaries, Campbell had journeyed to the Himalayas and was determined to grow his own Himalayan glades of rhododendron and azalea. In May and June each year the woodland sections of Arduaine Gardens are a riot of brilliant colour while in the sheltered hollows a fine water garden adds an air of tranquillity. What Arthur Campbell had begun on a treeless headland in 1897 was taken over and largely completed by the

Arduaine Gardens (*Author's Collection*)

Wright brothers during the middle part of the twentieth century. In the 1990s they in turn, handed the gardens into the keeping of the National Trust for Scotland. Today the gardens employ several local people in support of the Superintendent appointed from the Royal Botanic Gardens at Kew.

At the entrance to Arduaine Gardens stands Loch Melfort Hotel which was built in the 1980s to a traditional design. The two enterprises, operating in harmony, have done much to improve local prospects by increasing tourist interest in the area.

As for the remainder of the parish, housing is sparse along the deeply indented coastline, the steep-sided gullies and sharply contoured hills lending themselves to little other than grazing and forestation. It is only on the adjoining islands of Seil, Luing and Easdale, where the landscape becomes less daunting and the earth yields up its bounty, that there has been any substantial development in the past three hundred years.

4

KILBRANDON AND KILCHATTAN

Blue slates, chocolate-coloured cattle and a sailor priest

The parish of Kilbrandon and Kilchattan begins at the seaward end of Loch Feochan on the outskirts of the village of Kilninver and is almost surrounded by the Atlantic Ocean. It covers an area of approximately sixty square miles and takes in a part of the Degnish peninsula as well as a group of islands which are known as the Slate Islands of Netherlorn. Much of the highest ground in the parish has a covering of coniferous forest, planted during the 1950s and now reaching maturity. The remaining high ground is open country grazed by sheep and wild deer. In the deeper gullies are remnants of ancient oak woods while nearer the coast and along the river valleys more fertile ground is occupied by a number of farms once producing grain crops and flax but now given over mainly to raising cattle and sheep. Much of the coastline is rugged and dangerous where vertical cliffs are buffeted by the Atlantic waves, but there are many sheltered havens for mariners and flat, raised beaches left over from the last Ice Age provide level ground for a village or for cultivation.

The islands of Seil, Luing and Easdale lie only a short distance offshore and are so closely related to the mainland of Argyll both geographically and politically as to be included in this book. The two parishes of Kilbrandon and Kilchattan were amalgamated in 1835 but parish churches have been retained, Kilchattan on the island of Luing and Kilbrandon on Seil. Kilchattan parish includes the islands of Luing, Torsa, Shuna and surrounding small islands which are mostly uninhabited, while Kilbrandon encompasses the isles of Seil and Easdale and that part of the Degnish peninsula which includes Ardmaddy Castle and its policies. The island of Belnahua a little further offshore in the Sound of Lorn was included in the parish records of the Isle of Jura but is discussed here because of its relation to the slate industry.

The story of Kilbrandon and Kilchattan begins 600 million years ago when thick deposits of silt and mud were laid down in a shallow sea draining highland masses to north and south. These soft, malleable deposits, vulnerable to every movement of the techtonic plates which meet along the edge of Northern Europe, were compressed, heated and crumpled until they had become a solid rock whose crystalline components are so arranged as to form sheets or laminates. When freshly exposed to the air, slate rock can be easily separated into thin sheets and cut to the required size. It is light enough for building purposes but resilient in any climate. The distinguishing features of slate from the Easdale belt, which stetches from Jura north-eastwards along the Great Glen Fault to Inverness, are its blue colour and the abundance of crystals of iron pyrites, fool's gold, to be found particularly at the margins of the slate seams.

The life expectancy of a slate roof depends upon its origin; in the case of Easdale slate it seems infinite. There are buildings in Scotland roofed in the thirteenth and fourteenth centuries, the slates of which have survived although the timbers supporting them have been renewed, many times.

Thirty million years ago the Isle of Mull erupted in a volcano, Ben Mor, which spewed out its lavas like the spokes of a giant wheel, penetrating the surrounding rocks and finally covering vast areas of ground rock with a sheet of molten lava. Subsequent action of the sea, assisted by frost and wind, eventually eroded the volcanic material and exposed the underlying slate around the shores so that by the time Man appeared, it was ready and waiting to be utilised.

The discovery of carved bones and collections of sea shells, together with primitive flint tools found on the island of Shuna, indicate occupation of the parish of Kilchattan by hunter-gatherers of the Stone Age, as early as 5000 BC. Neolithic tribes, exploring the coast for safe havens, food and materials with which to construct their shelters, discovered the sheets of flat slate rock made a solid waterproof floor or a secure covering for the burial of the dead. A stone floor of Neolithic age (*c.* 3000 BC) which includes pieces of Easdale slate has recently been exposed near Oban and many cists in the area incorporate slate rock.

The contents of some cairns of the Neolithic period also indicate the presence of farmers and boatbuilders and the quantity of flint tools discovered on Shuna suggests trading, almost certainly by sea, with settlements far to the south. Shuna was also the site of a remarkable discovery of Bronze Age swords (*c.* 1500 BC), three of which, well preserved by the anaerobic conditions, were found projecting vertically upwards out of a peat bog. On the island of

Luing, cup markings of the same period have been discovered on a flat rock set into the portal of Dun Leccamore. Although the dun or hill fort dates from around the first century AD, it is thought the stone bearing these ancient markings may have been incorporated by the masons building the fort, because of its supposed magical properties. On the other hand they may just have fancied the decoration.

Iron Age hill forts abound in this area, situated on hills or steep cliffs, generally guarding an inlet or a narrow passage between two islands. Clearly any threat of invasion at this time came from the sea. So many small islands close to the mainland offered safe haven to mariners, easy access to fresh water and food and the added incentive of useful slabs of flat rock which could be carried away for a multitude of purposes. The name Luing implies a safe anchorage.

The oldest method of extracting the slate rock is dependent upon sea water and the tides. Slate rock exposed at low tide was attacked using wooden wedges hammered into natural cracks in the rock. These swelled when wet and forced the laminations apart. Using such primitive tools, the task must have been slow and laborious but nevertheless considerable quantities of rock had already been taken from the Slate Islands by the time the Scoti arrived from Ireland and landed on this coast intent upon subduing the native tribesmen of what was then Dalriada. The Scoti under their leader Loarn paved the way for missionaries who arrived in the middle of the sixth century.

Both St Brendan of Clonfert (in Galway) and St Cathan were contemporary with St Columba but Brendan had already established a cell in Netherlorn, thirty years before Columba reached Iona. Widely known as the navigator priest, St Brendan explored great areas of the North Atlantic during the sixth century and is thought to have reached Greenland. Some historians even suggest he was the first European to step ashore in North America. In his wanderings Brendan visited the coast of Scotland on many occasions and seems to have been particularly attracted to this part of Argyll. Around AD 550 he established his chapel close beside a Druidic stone circle which stands near the Dubh Loch, a small lochan to the west of the Duachy farmhouse and separated from the Clachan Sound by a ridge of high ground. The earliest Christian settlement in these islands, associated with this cell, became the village of Clachan which lies on the Isle of Seil at the narrowest part of the Sound.

St Cattan established his cell in the south of the island of Luing near Leccamore, an Iron Age hill fort. Subsequently a medieval church was built near the site serving a parish sparsely populated, its settlements presumably associated with the hill forts which had been built at strategic points along the length of the island. Luing, always a home of seafarers and fishermen as well as farmers was, in the eleventh and twelfth centuries, frequently visited by the Vikings.

When the slate industry on Easdale and Seil prompted an increase in population towards the end of the eighteenth century, this exceptionally fertile island was considered to be the larder for others in the group. Cattle were grazed on the lush meadow lands and grain for meal, animal feed and bere for the distillery, were all produced here. Flax and root crops were grown in the less exposed glens. There were several mills for the production of flour, one of which remains.

When slate quarries were eventually opened on Luing early in the nineteenth century, new villages were built in close proximity to the exposures. To the north of the island, St Mary Port consists of a small scattering of houses beside a quarry where the slate can still be taken from exposures above sea level.

In the far south of the island, near Leccamore and the remains of the ancient Kilchattan church, Toberonochy developed alongside a deep slate quarry which is now water filled. The well-sheltered bay and the proximity of the church suggest that this village may originally have been the principal settlement in the parish.

Only three walls of the twelfth-century parish church of Kilchattan remain, standing on a small knoll some 500 m north of Toberonochy village. Scratched on the outer walls of the church are graffiti depicting Viking galleys, geometric and human figures. The drawings are at a height suggesting they were made by children and the subject matter suggests they may be of the same period as the church itself. One can imagine the Early Christian spankings these youngsters might have received for their artistic expression!

Ancient tombstones with attractive and delicately carved symbols, abound here together with an interesting collection of names and inscriptions. On the west wall of the church a pair of panels commemorate one Alexander Campbell, a zealous Covenanter who suffered great humiliation for his convictions before his death in 1829.

In the newer part of the cemetery, alongside generations of islanders, are buried members of the crew of the Latvian vessel *Helena*

Faulbaums which sank off the coast of Belnahua in 1936. Among them is the wireless operator, Albert Sulcs, only nineteen years of age, who stayed at his post sending signals for assistance until the ship went down. Some of the crew were rescued and taken in by the people of Luing. Bodies of those who drowned were given Christian burial by the villagers. A moving description of the event is given in the *Oban Times* of the following week. Having been landed at Toberonochy from a boat transporting the dead from Belnahua and Cullipool, each of the coffins was carried by members of the crew and islanders through the silent village and up the hill to the burial ground where a service was held in the open air. The Latvian relatives of those who died still return to Luing for special anniversaries when they are entertained in the homes of the islanders. A memorial stone relating the tragic event was erected by the islanders and in the present parish church at Achafolla is a lectern presented by the Latvians to the people of Luing.

In 1835 the parishes of Kilbrandon and Kilchattan were united. The medieval church of Kilchattan having become ruinous, it was decided that a new church should be built at North Cuan on Seil to accommodate parishioners from both islands. One older resident, Angus Shaw, who spent his early life in Cullipool, recalls how the family would walk the two miles across the hills on a fine Sunday morning to the ferry landing.

The population of Luing never warranted the provision of more than one school for older children although schools for the very young were provided both at Cullipool and Toberonochy. The argument as to which village should have the new school, built in the 1870s to conform to the new Education Act, was solved diplomatically by building it in the centre of the island, at Achafolla. While this successfully assuaged territorial argument it meant that all the island children had a daily walk of up to three miles, each way. Angus Shaw remembers running to school barefoot through the heather rather than tramp along the road in his heavy boots! When in 1934 a new parish church was built, it too was sited at Achafolla.

Today Toberonochy is important for being the centre for the island's agricultural industry, the principal farm being that at Ardlarach, on Black Mill Bay. Built by order of the Earl of Breadalbane in the late eighteenth century, the farm was intended to supply grain and dairy products sufficient for the needs of the quarry workers in the district. The farmhouse, known as the Tacksman's House, is a three-bay, two-storey dwelling, built in 1787 by Patrick MacDougall. It was extended to an L-shaped plan early in the nineteenth century.

A short distance away from Black Mill Bay are the steadings and dwelling houses of Kilchattan Farm which originate from the 1840s when Breadalbane created a model farm along the lines of those at Inveraray. There are cattle byres for over-wintering the beasts, grain storage and a model dairy.

Until the late eighteenth century it was usual for cattle to be cleared from the farms in the Western Highlands and islands every autumn because the animals could not withstand the rigours of the winter climate outdoors and there was no means of keeping more than a few beasts under cover. The provision of cattle byres at Kilchattan Farm alleviated the problem to some extent but it was not until the 1940s that it was solved satisfactorily. Owners of the Luing farmlands since the 1940s, the Cadzo family has created its own breed of Luing cattle. The beasts have thick hides liberally covered in tightly curled, chocolate-brown hair. Because of their ability to withstand the rigours of a Western Isles winter, they are sought after by farmers working in similar climatic conditions, worldwide.

From the 1830s and for the next one hundred years, Black Mill Bay, a mile or so to the west of Toberonochy, was a port of call for the West Coast steamers and for the puffers delivering bulk cargoes, in particular coal and timber. There was a ticket office on the pier and a postal sorting office set up when, towards the end of the nineteenth century, postal deliveries from Glasgow were distributed from here to all parts of the Slate Islands.

Uncertainty about the future of the industry and a falling off in orders led to discontent amongst the quarrymen, culminating at last in a strike. For long the pages of the *Oban Times* rang with the opinions of those for and against the strikers. The start of the First World War finally put paid to endless comment and speculation. The quarries closed and the men joined the services or went to the shipyards and factories of the Clyde valley to work.

In the north-west of Luing, the village of Cullipool has a number of water-filled slate quarries as well as an extensive exposure above sea level. This latter is still worked on occasion by a few individuals seeking material for limited domestic requirements. Like other quarrying villages the houses here are sturdy, single-storey, two-roomed buildings, built of slate stone and dolerite whin, harled and painted white under a slated roof. To the south of the village is a

Cullipool slate quarry, *c.* 1880 (*Slate Islands Centre*)

small township overlooking the Fladda lighthouse and consisting of a number of late nineteenth-century villas built to accommodate businessmen associated with the quarries.

When in the 1860s demand for slate exceeded the capability of the quarriers to produce it, a team of men was brought to Luing from Balachullish to help out. Being dedicated Episcopalians, these men spurned the Presbyterian parish church and determined to have their own building. Their tiny church, a plain rectangular building with neat bell tower, stands on a knoll overlooking the village. It is now a private dwelling house.

In the 1880s, with the intention of subsidising the income of the quarrymen, Breadalbane established a lobster farm on the seashore by closing off waters surrounding a group of islets. In these pools lobsters caught during the main fishing season were kept and fattened for the Christmas and New Year markets when prices were at their highest. In the census of 1891 one resident on the island of Belnahua is described as a lobster fisherman, an occupation so specific as to suggest that it was his job to keep the lobster pools stocked up.

Cullipool today is occupied by professional fishermen, providers of accommodation and services for tourists, and agricultural workers.

Cullipool lobster ponds, *c.* 1900 (*Easdale Museum*)

Many of the houses are second homes or self-catering holiday cottages left vacant during the winter months. The village shop not only provides for most of the needs of the island's residents but also provides for holidaymakers and day-trippers. In the absence of a village pub, most entertainment takes place in private houses.

The Luing general store and the post office are the island's main meeting places. Many social activities, however, take place at Achafolla where the school and church provide suitable meeting rooms. Recently the islanders acquired lottery funding to renovate the old village hall at Toberonochy. Traffic now flows more freely between the villages, placing a considerable burden upon the island's only road.

The provision of a vehicular ferry has led during the twentieth century to an increase in the number of daily visitors and provided an opportunity for residents to seek employment off the island. In recent times discussions have taken place regarding the provision of a bridge between North and South Cuan. At present Luing looks inwards for its entertainment and finds within its number sufficient talent, musical, theatrical and artistic, to produce a rich and rewarding cultural life.

The village of Clachan on Seil first receives mention in ecclesiastical records as the place where John Campbell, Chaplain to King Robert I, was educated in the mid-thirteenth century. Little is known of Clachan in the intervening years but in the late sixteenth century

Ardfad Castle was built by the Campbell laird, a mile or two to the north of Clachan village on a rocky headland overlooking Insh Island. The establishment of such a prestigious dwelling would undoubtedly have increased the village population because the lairds in those times employed not only house servants and estate workers but also a small private army, all of whom, together with their wives and families, would have required shelter. Within 200 years Ardfad had fallen into ruin and today only vestigial footings of this medieval hall-house remain. It was replaced late in the eighteenth century by the present Ardencaple House, a laird's two-storey house with a turnpike stair to the rear. Sadly, the building's original fine proportions have been somewhat compromised by later, nineteenth-century, additions. A small township of workers' cottages grew up near the house providing accommodation for servants and estate workers but, as the nineteenth century Breadalbane estate records show, the majority of employees continued to reside in Clachan.

The village stands at the beginning of the only road through the Slate Islands and is linked to the mainland by a 200-year-old, humpbacked bridge. At this spot the waters of the Atlantic Ocean are no more than 30 m across even at the highest of tides. With a maximum tidal difference of some 4.5 m, it is possible to float a

Clahan Bridge (Bridge over the Atlantic), Seil, *c.* 1900 (*Easdale Museum*)

sizeable vessel under the arch of the bridge at high tide while being able to wade across from shore to shore when the tide is on the ebb. Indeed, before the bridge to Seil was built in 1791, a woman called Annie Bridges might have carried you across to the island, piggy-back, for a penny! The Clachan Bridge or the Bridge over the Atlantic, as this structure has become widely known, was built from a design of Robert Mylne, the architect to the 5th Duke of Argyll. The builders were the Stevenson brothers of Oban.

Clachan was from earliest times an important rallying point for cattle drovers bringing their stock to market from the inner isles. There is little doubt that an early change-house was established here, almost certainly on the very spot where the Tigh-an-truish Inn now stands. The census returns of 1791 record a brew-house in one section of the present complex of buildings. Beside it was a family of trouser-makers, a fact which may account for the name of the inn, Tigh-an-truish, (House of Trousers). The brew-house appears to have been extended at some time in the middle of the nineteenth century. The work must have been inferior because estate records show there followed many complaints concerning the use of defective materials and persistent leakages. In 1897 the Earl of Breadalbane ordered a complete refurbishment of the Tigh-an-truish. A new landlord was appointed, a Mr Weir, who remained until well into the twentieth century.

The village inn is at the hub of this small community which, although lacking a general store, can boast the only petrol filling station between the islands and Oban town centre. Until the late 1980s, a post office existed in Alma Cottage at the southern edge of the village.

Houses on either side of the bridge are mainly of late eighteenth- or early nineteenth-century date but there are a number of ruins which may be older. Several buildings have been substantially altered in recent years. There is no record of a church, but Ardencaple School, built in 1873, was still in use until it burned down in the 1950s.

With the general exodus from the area which took place during the first quarter of the twentieth century, the village population fell to an all-time low in the 1940s. Since then it has been growing steadily. With the expansion of industry and commerce in Oban and the increase in car-ownership, Clachan Seil has become a favoured location for commuters. Housing stock has been much improved in the past thirty years. Modern bungalows are arranged across the hillside, subtly disguised by stands of deciduous trees, while along

Tigh-an-truish Hotel

by Oban, Argyll

| Telephone Balvicar 242 | Proprietrix Miss F. MacLean | Seven-Day Licence |

Pamphlet advertising Tigh-an-truish Hotel, 1940s (*Slate Islands Centre*)

the roadside many of the houses, with the exception of a small development by the Local Authority, have been designed to blend in with the traditional architecture of the area. Most of the houses are permanent homes rather than holiday accommodation although some offer bed-and-breakfast during the tourist season. A small, late twentieth-century hotel completes the holiday provision in this part of the island.

For 200 years the Vikings harried settlements all along the western coast of Argyll but, maybe because of the heavily fortified shoreline, there is little evidence that they molested the inhabitants of Seil. There are, however, many tales of battles along this coast between the local lairds, the MacDougalls of Lorn, the Macdonalds, Lords of the Isles and the Macleans of Duart. It was not until Robert the Bruce was crowned King of Scotland in 1306 that there was any real attempt made to unify the clans. Robert solved the problem in Argyll by granting a large part of the territory and jurisdiction in the county to Sir Colin Campbell of Lochawe whose descendents were the Earls and

Dukes of Argyll and the Earls of Breadalbane. In 1479, Sir Duncan Campbell made a grant of lands at Ardmaddye to John McDowgall (MacDougall) of Rarey (Raera). Here the MacDougalls built the original Ardmaddy castle in a secluded ravine which opens out into a well-protected bay on the south-western shore of Balvicar Sound.

The Campbells and the MacDougalls were closely allied for the next two centuries, the relationship cemented by a series of marriages between the clans. Following the Reformation, however, the Campbells generally adhered to Protestantism while the MacDougalls retained their staunch Catholicism. When conflict arose between the two religious factions, the two families found themselves on opposing sides.

In 1648 John MacDougall of Rarey was imprisoned at Inverary, tried and found guilty of bigamy by the Marquis of Argyll. He was heavily fined and his property confiscated. Argyll handed the stewardship of the Ardmaddy policies to his Glenorchy cousins. From then until the early years of the twentieth century, the castle and most of the land associated with the parishes of Kilbrandon and Kilchattan remained in the hands of the Earls of Breadalbane.

The original Ardmaddy Castle was an oblong tower house of the late fifteenth century. This was reduced to a single storey, however, before the present structure was developed during the occupancy of Neil Campbell, in 1737. Wings have been added to the original tower extending both public and private rooms, while to the north-east of the house a separate court of offices was built between 1837 and 1839. The house bears the distinction of having two fireplaces uniquely constructed of Easdale marble, a small quarry in the castle grounds having given rise to some speculation when the Easdale Marble & Slate Quarrying Company was inaugurated in 1745. The marble proved to be non-commercial, however, and that part of the company's title was quickly dropped.

At the far end of the walled garden is a neoclassical stone bridge and a path leading to the family's burial ground with medieval memorials to members of both the MacDougall and Campbell of Breadalbane families.

In the 1920s the 4th Marquess of Breadalbane died without issue. While his widow was to occupy Ardmaddy until her death in 1933, the remainder of the vast Breadalbane estates were sold to pay off the family debts. Seil, Luing and Easdale were included in the sale but Easdale Island remained unsold until the 1950s. The 4th Marchioness is commemorated by the stained-glass windows which were created by the artist Douglas Strachan and can be found in the parish church of Kilbrandon on the Isle of Seil.

The earliest habitation recorded in the village of Balvicar, on Seil, is an Iron Age fort standing on a ridge above the village. On this site the foundation of at least one circular wooden house has been identified proving that people lived here at some time between 600 BC and AD 400.

The name Balvicar means the vicar's fields, indicating an early association with the church. The old burial ground on the south side of the village contains many ancient monuments and has exposed at its centre a part of the crypt of a medieval church possibly of the twelfth century. Despite having been described as being in a ruinous state at the beginning of the eighteenth century, this early Kilbrandon Church was probably in use until the building of the new parish church at Cuan in 1735. At some distance to the south of the village, near Kilbrandon House, are the remains of an even earlier chapel.

During the sixteenth and seventeenth centuries the Balvicar estate was owned by the Campbells of Calder, now represented by the Earl of Cawdor. Early in the sixteenth century, the infant Muriel of Cawdor was left an orphan. Having inherited the estates of the late Thane, Muriel was a very wealthy heiress. Anxious to get his hands on her money, her official guardian, the Earl of Argyll, planned to marry his ward off to his third son, John Campbell, thereby securing the Cawdor estates for the family.

The infant Muriel was removed to Inverary and in 1510 she was married to John Campbell. The couple, taking the title Campbell of Calder, were granted the Balvicar lands and Muriel remained on Seil until her death in 1575. In 1770 the Campbells of Calder exchanged their Balvicar property for land at Benderloch and Campbell of Breadalbane merged the village with his other holdings on Seil.

For several centuries Balvicar mainly supported the farming community on Seil and there was a considerable fleet of fishing vessels moored in Balvicar Bay. When in the late eighteenth century the Duke of Argyll established linen factories in many villages throughout Argyll, the marshy ground outwith the village was found to be suitable for the growing of flax and many cottagers were encouraged to become spinners and weavers.

The slate quarries at Balvicar were not opened until the middle of the nineteenth century when orders for slate could no longer be met solely by the Easdale and Luing quarries. They continued working for some time after the Easdale quarries closed down in 1912 and were reinstated in the 1950s for a short period to meet a specific demand during the post-war reconstruction of Glasgow.

The majority of Balvicar's cottages date from the early part of the nineteenth century and were built to the same pattern as those at Easdale and on Luing: two rooms were divided by a narrow lobby, store cupboard and a box bed. There was no sanitation and water was drawn from a standpipe at the end of the village street.

In his reports to the County Medical Officer in the 1890s, Dr Patrick Gillies, medical officer to the quarrying company, reports on the atrocious condition of the village and the noxious odours arising from the village midden. He describes an urgent need for a scavenging service to remove waste to a safe distance where it might be properly disposed of.

Balvicar village at the beginning of the twenty-first century benefits from two substantial developments of private housing which took place in the 1980s and 1990s. Employment has been provided by the establishment of a boatyard and chandlery servicing both working fishing boats and pleasure craft. A modern fish-processing plant established in the mid-1990s prepares locally caught shellfish and salmon for markets abroad, while on the Kilbrandon estate a mile or two to the south of the village, there is an oyster farm selling its produce to local restaurants and hotels as well as exporting to the Continent.

The village economy is also boosted by a number of holiday chalets which bring trade to the village stores and other local enterprises throughout the year. There is no school in the village now but for several centuries instruction was provided by the MacLachlan family of Kilbride in a schoolroom which occupied a site near the Balvicar cross roads. Both the Easdale Medical Practice and the new Manse, built in 1993, are situated nearby.

The parish church of Kilbrandon stands a mile or so along the Cuan road beyond the new cemetery which was opened during the 1980s. Built in 1864–6 by Alexander MacIntyre it is a simple Gothic Hall with a single gallery to the rear and an octagonal ogee-domed belfry above the west gable. The interior lighting is greatly enhanced by the striking stained-glass windows of Douglas Strachan, presented to the church in memory of the Marchioness of Breadalbane.

Kilbride Farmhouse, Seil, *c.* 1890 (*Easdale Museum*)

The small township of Kilbride lies along the Easdale road a mile or so north-west of Balvicar. Today it comprises a collection of holiday cottages and a farmhouse but it was once a substantial settlement associated with a fine mansion house, the home of the MacLachlan family.

In the early days of the Christian Church the MacLachlans had been noted clerics having a close association with Iona Abbey. Consequently at the Reformation, when the Abbey of Iona was threatened with dissolution, the MacLachlans were asked to take into their safe-keeping valuable manuscripts from the Iona library. These Kilbride Manuscripts were carefully hoarded at Kilbride House for many generations until, in the early years of the twentieth century, the head of the family placed them in the keeping of the Advocates' Library in Edinburgh.

Late in the seventeenth century, following a series of wet summers which had seriously depleted food supplies and left the people weak from starvation, plague visited the island of Seil. Many of the people of Kilbride died and were buried in a mass grave below the ancient hill fort of Cnoc an Tigh Mor to the west of the township. A cairn raised above the spot recalled this sad event, concluding with the words (translated from the Gaelic), 'It is a sad day when there are no welks to be had.' In times of hardship the islanders were reduced to gleaning what food they could from the seashore. Welks were their last recourse.

During the decades following the Disruption of 1843, small breakaway communities sought alternative accommodation for their worship. In the Slate Islands, the Free Church and the Covenanters each built churches of their own, the Covenanters at North Cuan and the Free Church at Balvicar. When in 1911 these two denominations decided to amalgamate, both abandoned their separate churches and together they purchased a pre-fabricated building in corrugated iron. The tin church which stands above the Kilbride farmhouse was finally abandoned when members of the United Free Church rejoined the Church of Scotland.

On visiting the Western Islands in 1549, Dean Munro reported the island of Belnahua as 'ane iyllane quharin there is fair skailzie aneuche', an island where there is a quantity of good slate. Of Eilean-a-beithich (Ellanabeich), the Isle of Birches, he says: 'quairein there is abundance of skailzie to be win'.

This, the earliest written reference to the Slate Islands, indicates that, as we have already seen, slate was being taken away from these islands for centuries before the Earl of Breadalbane and three of his kinsmen together formed the Easdale Marble & Slate Quarrying Company in 1745.

One rather unfortunate result of the tectonic movements which created the slate beds in the first place was a final heave sideways, buckling the beds and throwing up a series of enormous anticlines. As a consequence, the slate beds throughout the islands dive down into the ground at an angle of between 37 and 45 degrees. By the time the Breadalbane Campbells had decided to exploit this major resource on a commercial basis, all that remained above sea level was a steep escarpment of dolerite rock, a Tertiary volcanic intrusion from Mull, which had penetrated a natural fissure in the slate bedrock metamorphosing it a second time on either side, to a depth of up to a metre. This ultra-baked slate which has lost its laminations and is composed largely of quartz was described by quarrymen as bad rock and when they reached it they stopped quarrying. As a consequence, the village on Easdale Island nestles in the shelter of a small hill some 180 feet high. On it grows quite luscious grass and a few windswept bushes, providing fodder for the small herd of cattle which provided meat and milk for the 400 or so inhabitants of the island during the nineteenth century.

Since the quarriers were obliged to follow the slate beds almost vertically into the ground, there was a constant battle to keep water out of the workings. Various types of pumping apparatus were employed: a horse-gin, windmill and Newcomen's atmospheric pump were finally replaced by a steam-driven pump rescued from a sunken ship. This proved so successful that others were quickly introduced in all the quarries. From time to time it was decided the pumping system of the day could no longer cope with the depth reached. The quarry was then abandoned and another begun, elsewhere. When a more sophisticated pumping system was introduced, quarrying resumed in the discarded pits, to a lower level. Eventually some quarries reached depths of 70–80 metres below sea level! When, early in 1911, quarrying ceased and the pumps were withdrawn, the pits quickly filled with

Water-filled quarries, Easdale (*Author's Collection*)

water. Today most of Easdale Island and Belnahua are taken up with these deep pools, as are considerable areas on Seil and Luing.

As early as the thirteenth century, slate was used to roof major buildings throughout Scotland. Castles such as Ardmaddy, Dunollie, Dunstaffnage, Barcaldine and Stalker, belonging to the Campbells and their friends, and great churches such as Glasgow and Paisley Cathedrals were roofed in slates from Easdale. As the major cities began to develop during the sixteenth and seventeenth centuries, slate was in demand throughout Scotland, not only for roofing the most important buildings but also for the tenement homes of the working classes. By 1860, upwards of 7 million slates each year were being exported from the Slate Islands as far afield as Norway, Canada, the West Indies, and Australia. When members of the Free Church of Scotland emigrated to New Zealand in 1848 and settled in Otago in South Island, they took Easdale slate in their vessels as ballast and used it to roof the first churches in the new town of Dunedin. In the 1790s, 5 million slates per year were exported from Easdale. By the middle of the nineteenth century an annual total of 9 million slates was being exported from the combined quarries on the Slate Islands.

The eighteenth-century village on Easdale Island was a model of its day, with the houses sited in neat rows surrounding a substantial harbour which at one time contained a fleet of more than a hundred small craft of every kind. The Easdale men were skilled boatmen claiming many successes in the annual regattas.

Nothing was built on ground likely to yield commercial slate in the future so the houses themselves were clustered close together either on a whinstone (dolerite) base or along the edge of already existing quarries. As waste slate accumulated, this was used to infill disused quarries and to level the ground for further building.

At the peak of slate production on Easdale Island there were over 100 houses and 450 people, men, women and children lived in the village.

Other buildings on the island, several of which are now in a ruinous condition, were related to the actual slate operations. Included amongst these are a coalree by the harbour and an engine house, magazine, boiler house and smithy all located on the western side of the hill. Extremely skilled masons, the islanders built a massive sea wall of vertically placed slate stones, to protect the quarries to the west and north. They also built the eighteenth-century harbour and landing stage. A small section, some ten metres in length, is all that

Easdale quarriers all at sea (*Easdale Museum*)

remains of the old sea wall but much of the original harbour wall remains intact.

Islanders were allocated a small plot of ground which could be cultivated for root vegetables and cabbages but because there was no depth of soil on the island, they had to wait for Irish soil to be brought in as ballast by slate boats arriving from Ireland. This soil was spread across the individual plots which were separated by dry stone walls intended to give protection from the winds. The garden walls are still visible today and some residents have recently resumed cultivation.

To meet the day-to-day needs of the villagers, apart from the few cattle grazed on the hill and the 'back shore', sheep were kept on the uninhabited island of Insh a mile or two to the north. A correspondent recently described his boyhood on Easdale in the 1920s, recalling that every summer the shepherd would take his dog and row out to Insh for the shearing. In the autumn he collected a few sheep for market. It took a skilful man to row half a dozen of the woolly beasts in an open boat with only a dog to control them!

By the middle of the nineteenth century there was a company store where the villagers could obtain most of their requirements. The men were paid no more than once or twice a year and when the family's

Harbour and village, Easdale Island (*Author's Collection*)

money ran out, purchases were recorded on a large slate which hung on the wall of the shop (the origin of the expression to put it on the slate). The village had a bakery, a flesher (butcher), shoemaker and tailor and a sub-post office. Most of the women spun their own wool and knitted it into garments. Some wove their own woollen cloth. Locally grown flax was woven into linen fabric for underclothing and household use.

At different times throughout the period of industrial slate production, there were schools on Easdale Island and at one time there were more than forty children on role. The most substantial of all the school buildings, dated around 1870 and now a private house, stands close by the village hall.

In 1860 Easdale men formed the 1st Argyll Artillery Volunteers, setting up their battery of ex-naval cannon and museum pieces dating from the Peninsular Wars along the western shore of the island. As quarrymen, they were adept in the use of explosives and proved to be no mean gunners. In 1903 the Easdale Company won the King's Cup for small-arms firing in competition with regular troops.

The Volunteers built themselves a drill hall in the 1860s, a square building with a slated, pyramidal roof. This building served the islanders well as drill hall, a meeting place and for all kinds of

Easdale gunners, the Volunteers, *c.* 1880 (*Easdale Museum*)

indoor activities until, in the 1970s, it was converted for use as a fish-processing plant by the then owner of the island, Chris Nicholson. This enterprising gentleman was also responsible, together with local artist Jean Adams MBE, for setting up the Easdale Island Museum. In 2002 a substantial amount of Lottery funding was awarded for the restoration of the old drill hall, the work being completed in 2003. The original building has been sympathetically restored and extended to give every facility the community could have hoped for.

In the 1860s the Volunteers required a parade ground. Unfortunately on this island, with its deep pits in the ground and its mountains of waste slate, there was nowhere flat enough for marching and rifle drill. The answer was to fill in a section of the harbour. This meant that instead of being arranged around the water, many of the houses now surround three sides of the village green.

The slate industry began to fail at the beginning of the twentieth century and by 1911 the quarries on Easdale Island had been generally worked out. Quarrying continued elsewhere but the island population declined until, in the early 1950s, there was a handful of mainly elderly, permanent residents and a number of family-owned cottages which were visited occasionally during the summer months. A succession of enterprising island owners were to bring life back into the community with schemes to improve the economy and although none of these came to much the overall effect was a steady increase in the island's population which today amounts to approximately sixty permanent residents and some fifty more who regularly stay in their second homes. Any increase in housing stock is limited by the size of the island and the ability of its minimal infrastructure to cope with the demands of modern living. There has however been a steady improvement in existing housing, most of the eighteenth- and nineteenth-century buildings having been restored and extended in the past thirty years. The village is listed as a conservation area with many of the cottages B-graded. Its unique appearance is consequently protected and any further increase in population limited. Nevertheless, in the year 2002 Easdale was described as having the fastest growing island population in the whole of Scotland.

Until the nineteenth century, midway between Easdale Island and Easdale village on Seil lay the tiny *Eilean nam Betheich*, 'Island of the Birches'. This was once the location for a village for legend has it that in the days when the Macleans of Duart (on Mull) were rampaging along the coast, raiding the villages and stealing cattle and women, a man called McMarquis of Eilean nam Betheich, while visiting the Isle of Luing, spotted a galleon belonging to the Macleans heading for his home village. He swam the strait from south to north Cuan, battling against the fierce tidal race, ran along the cliffs to Dun Mor and awaited the galley. From his vantage point he rained down arrows into the pirate ship, killing all on board and saving his home from destruction.

During the last decades of the eighteenth century and well into the nineteenth century, this little island was completely quarried away at first to sea level and then deep below ground. Only a narrow lip of rock remained to keep out the seawater. Waste slate from this operation was systematically cast into the channel between the island and Seil Island until eventually the two were joined by a man-made causeway. It was upon the resulting made-up ground that three rows of neat little quarrymen's cottages were built in the early nineteenth century to create the village we see today. The quarry, which reached to a depth of eighty metres, was engulfed by a tidal wave on the night of 23 November 1881 at 4 a.m. Its sea wall was irreparably damaged.

Steamer at Easdale pier, 1890s (*Easdale Museum*)

Although for a time the men were out of work, they were eventually allocated to other quarries in the area. The quarries on Easdale Island were also swamped but could be pumped dry and were soon back in production. At the time, lurid tales were told in the press of drowning and loss of livelihood, none of which was substantiated. Nevertheless, many guides to the area still tell a highly embellished tale of woe!

In the 1870s, a pier was constructed on the Seil side of Easdale Sound for loading and unloading both passengers and cargo from the West Coast steamer which called twice daily on its route between Fort William and Crinan. This pier, sadly neglected and fallen into serious decay, is now disappearing a little at a time with every winter storm. In 2002 the Slate Islands Heritage Trust, fearful that it might at any time be cast into the sea, rescued the 130-year-old crane, once used for unloading cargo. After its refurbishment in the Glasgow yards of Alan Walker & Co., the Trust had the crane erected in the village square.

With direct access to the mainland by way of the Clachan Bridge, Easdale Village on Seil began to assume greater importance towards the end of the nineteenth century when the main post office for

Front Street, Ellenabeich, *c.* 1900 (*Easdale Museum*)

the Slate Islands was situated here and franked letters with its own, Easdale, postmark. The first telephone in the Slate Islands was installed in the post office on 16 March 1878 when villagers crowded into the tiny space to hear the voice of the Oban Postmaster speaking from sixteen miles away!

For many years the only hotel here was a temperance hotel but, on the end of a row of cottages eventually to form the foundations of the present An Cala House, there was a distillery. The stream which runs through the gardens is still known as the Distillery Burn.

A second Easdale company of Artillery Volunteers was raised in the village. Their firing range can still be seen on the side of Dun Mor. Outside the village stands the Volunteers' Drill Hall built *c.* 1870. An oblong building with pitched and slated roof, it has served the community well as a village hall for more than a hundred years.

The Quarry Manager, Angus Whyte, moved from Easdale Island in the 1870s when the Company built him a splendid new house on the edge of the village. In the 1890s, Breadalbane had this converted to a hotel. Although much altered and extended during the twentieth century, the Inshaig Park Hotel still displays many of its original late Victorian features such as marble floor tiles in the vestibule, a grand staircase and delicate plaster mouldings for cornices.

In 1876 a new school with schoolmaster's house was built on the outskirts of the village. With extensions and improvements, it is still in use today. Of similar age is Atlantic House, built as a manse to accommodate the minister of the combined parishes of Kilbrandon and Kilchattan. It was sold as a private dwelling house in the1990s when a new manse, purpose-built to fit the minister's modern-day requirements, was erected at Balvicar opposite the old burial ground.

A short distance along the road out of the village is Dunmore. Both house and farm are set well back from the road and sheltered below the steep-sided hill known as An Grinan. The stream running through the fertile meadows of Dunmore Farm is called Allt a'Mhuilin, the mill stream, suggesting the presence of a mill in the glen at some time in the past. Dunmore has been the location for an important dwelling house for many centuries. It is mentioned as early as the 1650s when the estranged wife of the incumbent of Ardmaddy Castle, John Maol MacDougall, took up residence there while her husband underwent a bigamous marriage with the sister of Campbell of Ardkinglas. This was a foolhardy decision on his part as it led to the imposition of a heavy fine of 2,000 guineas, a fortune in those times, and the forfeiture of all the MacDougall properties. From that time, Dunmore remained in the feu of the Campbells, eventually coming into the hands of the 1st Marquess of Breadalbane. In 1850, the Marquess let

Dunmore House, Easdale (*Author's Collection*)

Mid-twentieth-century Local Authority housing at Sea View, Easdale
(*Author's Collection*)

the farm and the dwelling house, to Dr Hugh Gillies, medical officer
to the Easdale Slate Quarrying Company. Of Gillies's large family,
his sons Patrick and Hugh both became medical men, Patrick taking
over his father's practice in the 1880s. The two Gillies doctors between
them cared for the health of the Easdale people from 1859 until 1912.
Patrick's brother, John Gillies, took over the running of the farm and
achieved considerable success in breeding cattle. Today's occupants
of Dunmore House are sheep farmers but they have also diversified,
raising game birds for the sporting fraternity, a small but important
aspect of the economy of the Highlands. Beyond Dunmore, at the foot
of Smiddy Brae, lies the tiny township of Sea View. Once consisting of
a collection of fishermen's cottages and an early nineteenth-century
manse, the population of this tiny settlement was doubled in the
1950s by the introduction of much-needed Local Authority housing.
Although mellowed by time, their sharp outlines subdued by salt
spray, these unsightly buildings seriously detract from the general
ambience of the district. Far more in keeping is the private scheme
developed at the southern end of Ellenabeich village in the 1990s.

Private housing development, 1990s, Ellenabeich (*Author's Collection*)

As on Easdale Island, the last remaining quarry in the village closed in 1911. At the outbreak of war in 1914, those unemployed quarrymen who had been members of the Easdale Volunteers, now the Territorials, were ready at once to go to war. Both Easdale Island and Easdale Village became ghost villages with just a few, mainly elderly folk remaining.

Between the wars, life was hard for those who had stayed behind while their relatives emigrated abroad or sought work in the Lowlands, but no harder perhaps than for those members of the family who suffered the indignities of the depression years in the cities. Only in the summer months did the villages come to life when family members returned to visit the old folks and filled the tiny cottages to bursting for a week or two.

At the start of the Second World War, many islanders joined the armed services while others went to the shipyards on the Clyde. The hostilities brought an influx of strangers to Oban although Easdale itself was affected very little. School records show that a few families returned as evacuees from the cities but seldom stayed for any length of time. The military activity taking place in Oban, however, meant plenty of work for the townspeople and an overspill of employment for the surrounding villages.

The engineer and designer, John Rollo, who had begun his first small operation in the old smithy at Kilbride township, now set up his business in an old quarry engine-house in the village. The Rollo works manufactured small-scale engineering lathes which could be easily transported and operated from within an army truck. By the end of the war Rollo's lathes were being used by engineers for repair work on every battlefront. After the war, the idea caught on in the DIY market but, regrettably, the demand for the product became too great for the small works at Easdale to handle and the business was forced to move away to the industrial Lowlands.

In the 1980s Easdale village on Seil officially changed its name to Ellenabeich to avoid confusion with the island and to give it a status of its own. Today it is largely a commuter village with a fair proportion of the cottages either second homes or given over to the self-catering holiday trade. A small restaurant and bar, together with a company running boat trips to the outer islands, provide a limited amount of work during the summer season but the largest employer in the village is the Highland Arts Studio, visited annually by hundreds of tour coaches bringing in thousands of visitors for a few hours at a time. The proprietor, C. John Taylor, poet, artist and composer, was an entrepreneur of extraordinary ability and a character well known in the district. His studio at Ellenabeich did much to promote tourism throughout Argyll and when he died in 2001 his family inherited both this and a number of similar, flourishing enterprises.

The village of North Cuan has long been established as the ferry access to the island of Luing and it was also the location of the parish church during the eighteenth and nineteenth centuries. The people residing here were generally engaged in fishing, agriculture, operation of the ferry and a number of activities peripheral to the real business of the parish which was the winning and exporting of slates. One family of weavers produced woollen cloth for making blankets for the entire community.

The old parish church, built at Cuan in 1835 when the parishes of Kilbrandon and Kilchattan were united, was deliberately sited in a position central to all the Slate Islands. Many of the parishioners arrived for Sunday worship by sea in their own small boats. At certain states of the tide the waters flow very strongly through the Cuan Sound. Nineteenth-century visitors described how a fleet of boats, quarrymen and their families from Easdale, Belnahua and Luing arrived at the church while the tide, flowing in a north to south direction, carried them along with the least amount of effort. The minister arranged his sermon to coincide with the change in the tidal flow so that the return journey was equally without effort!

In the village of North Cuan there was insufficient land available to build a manse. Instead, Breadalbane granted land for the purpose a mile or two to the north-east. As there was no suitable access road from the new manse, the minister too was obliged to make his way back and forth to church by sea. The 1735 manse, much extended and modernised, is now Kilbrandon House, purchased by Lord Kilbrandon as a family home in the 1970s.

The parish church at Cuan was replaced in 1866 by the present Kilbrandon Church on the Cuan Road. The old church was left empty for many years until in the 1890s Dr Patrick Gillies, after a long tussle with the authorities, converted it into a small isolation hospital. By this time the quarries were beginning to fail and there was considerable poverty in the parish. Poor food, inadequate clothing and overcrowding in the ill-ventilated cottages had created a situation in which contagious disease might spread like wildfire through the villages. The doctor felt he could control the situation if fever patients were isolated from their families. The hospital had accommodation for a full-time nurse and two small wards, one each for men and women. The church/hospital was eventually sold as a private dwelling house early in the twentieth century but it can still be distinguished by its original birdcage bell tower, retained despite extensive alterations.

Today as well as housing two ferry men and their families, Cuan is home to a number of folk engaged in arts and crafts activities. With a very small population to support them there are no longer any of the usual village services.

The tiny village on the island of Belnahua has long been deserted. Bravely the roofless buildings continue to present their gable ends to the Atlantic gales but with the destruction by winter storms of the only jetty offering a safe landing, they remain largely unvisited. It was a very different story during the nineteenth century when this tiny scrap of rock, standing alone in the middle of the Sound of Lorn, was the source of most of the roofs in Oban and the surrounding district.

Early in the nineteenth century the Stevenson brothers of Oban who were largely responsible for the construction of the town, leased the island and developed the quarries. At the peak of slate production which occurred in the 1860s, there were fifty-three men employed in

Deserted village of Belnahua (*Author's Collection*)

the Belnahua quarries including a blacksmith and an engineer. The Quarry Manager and his family lived in Belnahua House, the only two-storey building on the island. The remainder of the inhabitants lived in two rows of single-storey houses on the rims of the two quarries.

With forty-one children of school age a proper schoolhouse had to be built and a teacher engaged. There was no church on the island. In inclement weather the islanders worshiped in the school room, otherwise they sailed to the parish church at North Cuan.

One of the greatest problems of living on Belnahua was the complete absence of a natural supply of water for domestic purposes. Drinking water was carried across from Luing where a particular burn at Cullipool was reserved for the sole use of the Belnahua residents. Rainwater was caught in cisterns for quarry operations and wooden butts collected water from the roofs of the houses. Nevertheless there was little infectious disease on the island and reports of the late eighteenth century described octogenarians as still hale and hearty. A ninety-year-old woman was still able to thread her needle without the aid of spectacles!

At the outbreak of the First World War, the quarrymen downed tools and joined the armed forces, leaving their womenfolk to keep the pumps going until they came back. The women found that first winter without their men too much to bear and by the following spring the island was deserted. Items remain to this day on the floor of the water- filled quarry where the men abandoned them at the end of their final day's work. Trucks stand upon the rail track filled with slate rock awaiting the splitter's hand and steel tools, well preserved in the absence of oxygen, are strewn across the ground. For long the schoolroom remained intact complete with slates and slate pencils, desks and easel and many houses still retained their larger pieces of furniture.

The people never returned but because of the long time which elapsed before anyone thought to collect memorabilia which would have helped to establish a true picture of life on this desolate island, everything had either been looted or destroyed. The present owner of the island, a descendent of the family which leased and eventually purchased Belnahua, has a holiday home on the island of Luing and visits Belnahua infrequently. He plans, however, to retire to the island and try to farm it. Left to itself the village with its man-made brackish pools is a haven for wildlife and a place of extraordinary tranquillity and natural beauty.

5

KILMORE AND KILBRIDE

*From caves to castles: the MacDougalls of Dunollie
and Campbells of Lorn*

The parish of Kilmore and Kilbride stretches from Loch Etive in
the north to Loch Feochan in the south. To the east it is bounded
by Loch Nell and Loch Gleann-a-Bhearach and in the west by the
Sound of Lorn. Oban, the only town between Campbeltown and
Fort William on the west coast of Argyll, lies within the parish
boundaries.

The earliest evidence of settlement in the parish dates from 7000–
5000 BC. Cave and lake dwellings, duns and stone circles abound and
because of the abundance of relics of the Stone Age, delicately carved
bone harpoons, flints and other implements, Oban has lent its name,
Obanian, to the archaeological period in which they occur.

The earliest human deposits in the parish occur in caves exposed
by the falling sea levels following the last Ice Age. In 1791 the parish
minister, reporting in his Satistical Account of that year, described the
discovery of a cave in Glenmore Road near Carding Mill Bay which
contained a collection of human bones and skulls. Subsequently,
throughout the nineteenth century other caves were explored, each
yielding in particular bones both human and animal but it was
not until late in the twentieth century that these remains could be
accurately carbon dated. The Druimvargie rock shelter in Glenshallach,
found behind a tenement building of that name, yielded the oldest
artefacts, probably from 7800 BC. Few of the caves are easily accessible
and those which are have little now to show of past habitation. One
cave, discovered in 1890 to contain a few such relics, is sited in the cliff
beside the Oban Brewery and is included in that company's visitor
tour (the Distillery Cave). Recently an archaeological dig was carried
out in Glenshallach preceding a substantial housing development, but
disappointingly it yielded very little.

The spoil heaps of the Oban caves and the occupation layers
consisted of large collections of seashells, charcoal and ash from
fires, wild animal bones and vegetable refuse which suggest that the

occupants were hunter-gatherers rather than herdsmen or farmers. Neolithic and Bronze Age relics have been found at Raschoille and Carding Mill Bay including stag horns modified to form implements and flint arrow heads. There is little doubt that by this time the people were trading to the south where flint, unobtainable in Argyll, could be had for barter. A flint knife and arrowhead were found amongst sherds of Bronze Age pottery at Ardantrive on the island of Kerrera. These have been dated *c.* 2500 BC.

Around 3000 BC, Lorn was inhabited by farmers as well as the hunter-gatherers of earlier times. These Neolithic peoples, who had no metal and were obliged to import flint and stone for cutting implements, were nevertheless able to build boats large enough to ferry their domesticated animals from place to place and constructed monuments in the form of standing stones and burial cairns which have survived to this day. Above the village of Kilmore, overlooking Loch Nell, stands Dalineun, a pair of multi-chambered cairns where both Neolithic and later Bronze Age relics have been found, suggesting that the place was in use over a very long period. To the north and south of the cairn at Dalineun are no less than ten Bronze Age cairns stretching in a line over two kilometres in length. These probably date from *c.* 1500 BC. North of Loch Nell on the approach to Glen Lonan is a single standing stone, Diarmid's Pillar. Excavated in 1967, this was found to be standing within a circle of extra large boulders and is described as a kerb cairn. A number of other similar cairns have been found in the district.

Long before Christian missionaries arrived from Ireland, the original inhabitants of Lorn, the Picts, had been overwhelmed by Celts from Northern Europe who had arrived, either via England or Ireland, about 700 BC. The Celts brought with them their own culture and religion, introducing advanced craftsmanship in the form of stone buildings, brochs and duns or hill forts, and finely carved monuments to the dead which depict the natural world of birds, beasts and plant life. During the first centuries AD, the clan system developed with its overlords or chieftains and their kinsmen/followers. These warlike tribal groups took over sites of ancient hill forts and built their own strongholds. Apart from myth and legend, little is known of the very earliest years of the clan system but when, during the thirteenth and fifteenth centuries respectively, the MacDougalls built the present Dunstaffnage and Dunollie castles in the north of the parish, it was upon already existing, much earlier foundations. During the fifth

St Bean's Parish Church, Kilmore (*Author's Collection*)

and sixth centuries AD, the Scoti from Ireland made many forays to suppress the land they called Dalriada so that by the time the Irish Saints arrived on the scene at some time in the mid-sixth century much of Dalriada was already in the hands of the Scoti.

With such a wealth of prehistoric sites in a small area, it is hardly surprising that on arriving at the head of Loch Feochan in the sixth century AD, the Irish Saints should have chosen Kilmore as a suitable place for a cell.

Until Oban became a burgh in 1811, the village of Kilmore, four miles south of Oban, was the centre of parish activity. The ruins of a medieval church stand about a mile from the present church, on the outskirts of the village which is now bypassed by the road from Oban to Campbeltown. The church was dedicated to St Bean and is first mentioned in ecclesiastical records of the fourteenth century. When the parishes of Kilmore and Kilbride were united early in the seventeenth century, the church building was remodelled, the stone for this and later work being a green sandstone of Old Red Sandstone age quarried locally at Barnacarry. When in 1876, to meet the needs of the two villages of Kilmore and Kilbride, a new church was constructed alongside what is now the A816, the ancient church of St Bean had its roof dismantled and some walls deliberately demolished to give it the appearance of a romantic ruin.

In the St Bean churchyard are some fine examples of medieval gravestones of the Loch Awe School but the first legible name recorded is that of James Campbell, minister of Kilmore, who died in 1756 aged forty-seven years. The table tomb of Malcolm MacPherson, shepherd and Midmun who died in 1840 deserves special attention. A Midmun or Midman was a negotiator, an ombudsman of his day. One may picture the villagers of Kilmore calling upon the wise old shepherd to settle all their arguments. Today Kilmore is largely a residential dormitory with just a few people employed in agriculture and tourism, but it has its own church and community hall, a hotel, and a sub post office.

Close to the village of Lerags, which lies south of Oban, sandwiched between Loch Feochan and the Sound of Kerrera are the remains of the old parish church of Kilbride. A church, dedicated to St Bridget, is first recorded in the parish of Kilbride in 1249 when it was granted to the see of Argyll. Until the Reformation, the parish of Kilbride which included Kerrera and all the territory lying between Loch Feochan and Loch Etive was separate from the parish of Kilmore. The ruins which remain indicate that the church building underwent extensive reconstruction during the seventeenth and eighteenth centuries and even as late as 1842 considerable alterations were carried out by Peter MacNab, an Oban joiner. With a declining population enticed by the attractions of better employment to be had in the burgeoning town of Oban, it became necessary to merge the two parishes. Both parish churches were in need of considerable improvement so the decision was taken to build a new church on the present-day site.

The medieval church of Kilbride is traditionally the burial site of the MacDougalls of Lorn and the oldest decipherable monument in the graveyard is the table tomb in the MacDougall family's enclosure, to John MacDougall of MacDougall and Dunollie, who died in 1737 having been deprived of his lands following the Jacobite rising of 1715. Within the graveyard are several tombstones of the fourteenth and fifteenth century belonging to the Loch Awe School of carving.

By an Act of Privy Council in 1496, James IV required the first son of all Scottish gentry to attend school from age eight or nine years. In the township of Kilbride was one of the one hundred schools in Scotland at that time. It is likely that the sons of many important families in Argyll studied here.

At Ardoran, on the north shore of Loch Feochan, a little to the south of Kilbride, stood the home of the O'Conachers. This was a MacDougall sept of Irish origin who were hereditary surgeons in Lorn from before 1560 when John MacConacher paid the Earl of Argyll the sum of forty merks for the privilege of setting up his medical practice in Lorn. In 1621 Duncan Onacher of Ardoran is recorded as being 'mediciner in Lorn' and in 1662, Donald Onacher was the surgeon. The family seem to have lost their fixed base in 1793 when one Neil MacCulloch, dykebuilder, was at Ardoran.

Today the settlements at Kilbride and nearby Lerags consist of a scattering of farms and houses. There is no school or church and the inhabitants depend upon Oban for the bulk of their supplies. The economy of the glen depends largely upon farming and tourism.

Of all the Scottish clans, in this part of Scotland the MacDougalls and the Macdonalds can claim to be among the oldest. The history of their creation gives an insight into the governance by which Scotland has developed to the present day. The clan system was based upon blood ties and kinship. Members of a clan adopted the name of their laird. This post was generally hereditary although a laird without an heir might nominate his successor. If, however, a laird died without naming his heir, senior members of the clan elected their leader. The clan was a closed community, only the chief being allowed to marry outside it. This was intended to ensure a healthy blood line but also was a satisfactory means of acquiring additional goods and territory. Designed perhaps to bring unity and resolve old arguments, such marriages were just as likely to create tensions between the clans and begin a long standing feud.

Somerled, Lord of Lorne and King of the Southern Isles, was succeeded in 1164 by his son, Dugal who gave his name to the clan MacDugal (MacDougall). In the twelfth century, the MacDougalls held charter to the lands of Argyll from the present-day Kinlochleven to Crinan and from Taynuilt to the sea. They also held lordship over the islands of Mull, Tiree, Col, Jura and the small islands in the Sound of Lorn, Lismore and Kerrera. Stemming as it does from Dugal, son of Somerled, the Clan MacDougall preceded the Clan Macdonald by a full generation, the Macdonalds having sprung from a grandson of Somerled.

It was their vast holdings amongst the islands and their extensive coastline which encouraged the MacDougalls to build fine sailing ships which were manned by brave and expert seamen. Both the MacDougalls and their cousins the Macdonalds of the Isles, had fleets of galleys, each carrying some forty men. So swift and manoeuvrable were these vessels that they could outstrip anything the English or Europeans could send against them.

To the north of Oban stand two famous monuments to the great Clan MacDougall. These are the ruined Dunollie Castle, its accompanying Manor House and surrounding village, and Dunstaffnage Castle which was occupied until the mid-twentieth century and has been carefully restored by Historic Scotland.

Close beside the existing Dunstaffnage Castle is Sean Dun (Old Fort), the remnant of a very early fortification on this site. Duncan, Lord of the Isles began building Dunstaffnage early in the thirteenth century and most probably it was completed by his son Ewan. Of a sophisticated design comparable with the Norman castles in Wales and northern England, Dunstaffnage has stood the test of time very well. The original curtain walls and angle towers are still intact and internally many structures are still easily recognisable. The solid curtain wall with only one entrance made the building virtually impregnable and in all its long history the castle was only ever taken by siege.

Dunstaffnage occupies a commanding position at the mouth of Loch Etive, overlooking the Firth of Lorn. It guards the access, via Loch Etive and the Pass of Brander, into the heart of Scotland. In 1309 the castle fell to Robert the Bruce who placed it in the safe-keeping of the Campbells of Loch Awe. In 1388 the Lordship of Lorn was conferred upon the Stewarts and with it, responsibility for the upkeep of Dunstaffnage. Following the murder of John Stewart at the hands of the MacDougalls in 1463, the castle was again taken over by the MacDougalls for a short period. In 1470 Dunstaffnage was returned to Colin, the 1st Earl of Argyll, and has remained in Campbell charge ever since.

Dunstaffnage Castle, now in the care of Historic Scotland, has seen many structural changes in its long history. During the fifteenth century, soon after the accession of the Campbells, a gatehouse was added, while in the eighteenth century a straight forestair was constructed leading to a round-arched entrance cut into the curtain wall. In 1725 a small dwelling house was raised on the site of the original kitchens, for the use of the Captain and in 1903–4 the gatehouse was restored with garret gables, dormers and turret added. This provided lodging for the Captain and his family until, in 1958, the castle was placed in the hands of the Secretary of State for Scotland.

Close by the castle stands Dunstaffnage chapel which was built in 1240 for the benefit of the castle and those dwelling around it. As with all castletouns a settlement here would have housed the servants and warriors of the castle's Captain. The remains of the chapel indicate an advanced style of architecture with round-arched double windows, delicate stone carving and the slender supporting members reminiscent of the Early English period. Attached to the east gable is the Campbell burial aisle which was added in 1740 and contains numerous commemorative slabs and stones.

Although little trace remains of a village here, the Dunstaffnage Mains Farm probably occupies the site of an earlier township. The nearby village of Dunbeg was created during the Second World War to house military personnel associated with the various naval and air/sea rescue activities operating out of Oban Bay. After the war the housing was brought into public use, shops and a school were added and the large complex of naval workshops and offices became the foundation of the research establishment of the Scottish Association for Marine Science (SAMS) for which Dunstaffnage is known world-wide. While maintaining its status as a marine research establishment, Dunstaffnage has recently become an outpost of

Dunbeg, built 1940s (*Statistical Account, 1961*)

the University of the Highlands, the headquarters of which are at Inverness. This is a welcome answer to a long-felt need for local access to Higher Education.

Dunollie Castle was built by the MacDougalls, Lords of Lorne in the fifteenth century, to replace Dunstaffnage as their family seat. A Gaidhealtachd castle guards the narrow channel between Oban and the island of Kerrera. Because of its commanding position it is most surely built on the site of much earlier fortifications. A four-storey stone tower, now roofless, remains standing amid dense undergrowth. The two mural stairs survive but the once impregnable courtyard wall was opened in the sixteenth century to allow for a larger gateway.

In the seventeenth century the MacDougalls forsook the castle for a more convenient mansion, the present Dunollie House, begun in 1746 with its north range. The wings were added to the west and east flanks in 1834–5. The house was more recently restored by Leslie Graham MacDougall to provide a well-proportioned, unpretentious manor house. The policies of Dunollie Castle would have housed a township accommodating the MacDougall kinsmen but this lost its individuality as nineteenth-century development encroached upon the limited amount of flat ground at sea level to the north of Oban. Now Victorian and Edwardian villas and small hotels line the shore road from Oban Esplanade to Gannavan Sands.

Apart from the strongholds of Dunollie and Dunstaffnage, the MacDougalls built a third castle on Kerrera in 1582. This replaced a former fortification which had held a significant place in Scottish history. Gylen has the distinction of being chosen as the venue for a number of important conferences between the King of Scotland and his counterpart of Norway. Because of his links through marriage to each of the monarchs, the MacDougall Chieftain was considered a reliable host by both parties. It was at Gylen Castle in 1286 that King Alexander III died and was succeeded by his niece, Margaret, the infant Maid of Norway. The Maid was destined to be the bride of the infant son of Edward I of England, thereby securing a union between England and Scotland. The tragic death of the young queen only four years later gave rise to a long and bloody struggle for power in which the MacDougalls found themselves in a dilemma. Not knowing where to place their alliegance, with Hákon of Norway or John Balliol, his Scottish rival, Lord MacDougall finally supported the Scottish claimant. When Balliol surrendered his throne to Edward I of England, the clan switched allegiance to the new Scottish claimant, Robert the Bruce, Lord of Annandale. Sir Alexander MacDougall's wife was the sister of John Comyn, whose son, generally called the 'Red' Comyn, was stabbed to death by Bruce in Greyfriars Church, Dumfries, in 1306. This murder fired a new wave of confrontation between the clan and the powers behind the throne. Bruce was defeated by MacDougall at the battle of Dalrigh, near Tyndrum, but evaded capture. On Bruce's discarded cloak was found a magnificent example of Celtic jewellery and the 'brooch of Lorne' has remained, intermittently, in the possession of Clan MacDougall to the present day.

On the northern border of the parish stands Connel, one of the longest-established settlements in Argyll, having grown up around the ferry landing on the southern shore of Loch Etive. Connel ferry was important to travellers from earliest times, providing the narrowest crossing of Loch Etive at its seaward end, on the route between Fort William and Inveraray. It was crucial to the movement of troops, being one of the few places where cattle thieves might be intercepted as they moved their stolen herds across country and was used, from the fifteenth century onwards, by drovers bringing cattle and sheep to the trysts at Falkirk.

The ferryman's cottage by the shore was joined in due course by a stance for drovers and a few houses for those providing services to passing travellers. It was not until the late nineteenth century, when the railway made travel into Oban a matter of minutes rather than hours, that the middle classes chose to commute into Oban to work while spending their leisure time in the fashionable new development beside the beautiful Falls of Lora.

Much of the late Victorian housing in Connel is of very high quality and the splendid church of St Oran pays tribute to the generosity of its parishioners who contributed to its construction in 1887. The gable-ended cruciform structure with a square central tower is reminiscent of Iona Abbey, although in this case the tower seems excessively bulky and out of proportion. The church is richly endowed with late Victorian stained-glass windows.

At about the same period, a village centre of more modest buildings arose to house those providing services for the new inhabitants. A village shop, post office and a school were provided. A number of other establishments, providing goods and services, have come and

Connel Bridge, *c.* 1910

gone as travel arrangements to Oban improved. The original drovers' inn has been replaced by some splendid hotels while along the loch shore there is a number of late Victorian houses of distinction. The village school dates from the 1870s.

Visitors approaching Connel from any direction cannot fail to be impressed by their first view of the extraordinarily graceful lines of the Connel Bridge, constructed in 1902–3, to carry a branch railway line from Oban to Fort William. It is the second-largest cantilevered bridge in Britain. The line was never completed but it carried goods and passengers between Oban and Ballachulish for nearly seventy years before being axed in 1966 during the Beeching débâcle. Soon after its construction, however, it was realised that the bridge ought to have been designed to carry road traffic as well as rail. A form of tram was devised to run on the rails and carry pedestrians back and forth to North Connel. For a time flat rail cars were utilised to carry road vehicles across but once it became clear that the railway itself carried insufficient traffic to make the line profitable, one rail track was removed and a metalled roadway substituted, the trains continuing to run, but in either direction on the same rails. Today only road traffic uses the bridge with traffic lights to control the flow, in one direction at a time.

The author makes no apology for including Oban amongst the villages of north Argyll, for the speed of its development within the space of fifty years, from small township to chartered burgh and market town, is a phenomenon which is worth further consideration. When Thomas Pennant made his visit in 1769 he described Oban as a straggle of cottages situated along what is now Shore Street. James Boswell describes an agonising journey from Taynuilt to Oban along dangerous cliffs in the pitch dark, the road presumably following the coast via Dunstaffnage and Dunollie. In addition he mentions only two primitive inns in Oban, both patronised by cattle drovers.

Nine years earlier, Oban had come to the notice of the Customs and Excise Office. Tobacco was being imported from America, some of the cotters being employed in 'spinning' it before it could be sold on to the Lowland cities. A number of illicit stills operated in the area, supplying the whisky requirements of the locals and passing trade. Added to these activities there were suspicions of widespread smuggling. The only office of the Excise men on the north-west coast of Scotland was at Fort William, forty miles to the north. Unable to keep tags on the nefarious activities of the Lorn seamen, Customs officers demanded a new establishment closer to the seat of trouble. In 1758 a Customs House was built at the southern end of Shore Street close to the present south pier. This was demolished in 1880 to make way for the new railway.

In 1773 Ann Grant, the niece of the Revenue Officer, Colin MacVicar, kept a journal of her visit to Oban and waxed lyrical about the beauties of Oban Bay. She records that the total population of the whole parish, including Kilmore, Kilbride, Connel and Oban, 'is no more than 400 souls'. Also in 1773 the village was visitied a second time by Boswell and Johnson who had crossed from Mull in a flat-bottomed cattle-boat with brushwood strewn on deck for the comfort of the beasts. They stayed at the more salubrious of the two inns in the town at the corner of High Street. The second establishment was situated in Airds Crescent on the site of the present Aulay's Bar.

The town of Oban owed its development in part to the coming of traders from Glasgow who set up businesses exploiting local productions such as tanned leather, whisky and timber. Principally, however, it was two young men from Dunbartonshire, John and Hugh

Oban, a sketch by A. Stanley, 1876 (*Author's Collection*)

Stevenson, who were responsible for the rapid growth of this village towards the end of the eighteenth century.

When the Stevensons arrived in Oban, about 1776, they set themselves up with a shipbuilding yard, erected the Oban distillery and were widely employed as masons. At that time the lands to the south and west of the Black Lynn were owned by the Duke of Argyll while a Campbell of Dunstaffnage had built a dower-house at Glen Cruitten in 1667, its estate bordering the Black Lynn to the north. In 1778, John Stevenson took a lease on Glenshallach from the Duke and in 1779, Hugh leased Glen Cruitten from Campbell, both of them with a view to building houses and commercial property to accommodate the growing number of people wishing to set up in Oban. All the buildings of this period are of stone under slated roofs. In order to ensure a steady supply of roofing slates, the Stevensons purchased the island of Belnahua in the Sound of Lorn and opened a quarry there. Stone for the building programme was quarried locally probably at Barnacarry,* Ardentallen and even Oban itself.

Commercial properties were an integral part of the plans for development. Following their building of the distillery, the Stevensons

---

* This Barnacary is situated to the east of Kilmore and is not to be confused with the township of the same name near Kilninver on the way to Seil Island.

Free Church, Oban, built 1876 (*Author's Collection*)

constructed a tannery. This was followed by a more superior style of housing and a number of hotels. The Charter making Oban a burgh of barony was confirmed in 1820 and the first church was erected in 1821 at the southern end of Combie Street. Rebuilt in the 1890s, this is now the parish church of Kilmore and Oban and has taken over much of the responsibility for the parish from the earlier building at Kilmore. Following the Disruption of 1843, the individual factions in the burgh set up their own places of worship and Baptist, Episcopalian, Unitarian and Free Presbyterian Churches followed. The small Roman Catholic population in the parish at that time erected a prefabricated building which, because Oban was appointed as the centre for the Bishopric of the Isles, claimed to be the only corrugated-iron cathedral in the whole of Britain. It was not until the mid-twentieth century that work began on the present-day cathedral at the north end of the Esplanade. It is an indication of the huge influx of people into the new burgh that the church in Argyll Square, now a centre for Argyll and the Isles Tourist Board, was built to accommodate English-speaking members of the Free Church of Scotland. Until the middle of the nineteenth century, Gaelic was the language of the common people.

Former Oban High School, Rockfield Road, built 1876 (*Author's Collection*)

Hospitals and schools followed during the final decades of Victoria's reign. Oban High School was opened in Rockfield Road in 1876. It soon became clear that this, the only secondary school serving the whole of Argyll from Ardnamurchan to Campbeltown, including many of the islands, would require a larger building.

The present High School was erected in Soroba Road in 1890 and extended in 1897. Substantial additions were made after the Second World War and during 2001 the 1890s part of the building was demolished and rebuilt. The blue-painted Victorian cupola which stands at the front of the main entrance is all that remains of the original school. Even as recently as the 1890s, correspondence from Argyll Council concerning the new school building referred to the High School to be built in the village of Oban.

From the younger son of Sir Duncan Campbell of Lochow, Sir Colin Campbell of Glenorchy (1400–78), were descended the Earls and Marquises of Breadlbane. In Lorn, the Breadalbanes concentrated most of their energies upon their property in the Slate Islands. Like his predecessor, the 2nd Marquis, who had taken over the slate quarries in the 1840s and made them famous throughout the world, the 4th Marquis was a man of great vision, determined to avail himself of any opportunity to improve the value of his possessions. Together with his cousin, the Duke of Argyll, he invested vast sums of money in road construction and bridge building throughout the county and was one of the chief instigators in bringing the railway to Oban. His name appears at the head of any list of contributors to the building of churches, schools and hospitals in the parish and he made large investments in the tourist trade by upgrading the old drovers' inns along the route to Oban.

What the MacDougalls began within the parish, the Campbells carried on to the benefit of all. With swords sheathed, the two clans today work side by side for the benefit of the entire community. A glance at the telephone directory for the area is sufficient to convince us that despite the worldwide distribution of the two families, there are still plenty of both around to carry on the good work in the parish of Kilmore and Kilbride.

6
MUCKAIRN AND KENTALLEN

*Canon balls for Nelson and
electricity to power a nation*

To the south of Loch Etive are the parishes of Muckairn and Kilchrenan which include the villages of Taynuilt, Bonawe, Inverawe, Lochawe, Kilchrenan and Dalavich. Some of these villages date back to the sixth century and before, others owe their existence to twentieth-century investment in Argyll's economy.

Taynuilt, the most important settlement in the parish, is probably the oldest. It lies at the foot of Ben Cruachan a short distance from the southern shore of Loch Etive and once comprised a number of crofting hamlets bordering the road to the coast.

The present name of the parish and its church, Muckairn, is generally translated as the plain of cairns. Remains of Neolithic cairns, barrows, standing and cup stones in the district, in particular along the sides of Glen Nant and Glen Lonan substantiate this claim. There is also evidence of Celtic defences in the form of hill forts, along the road south to Kilchrenan.

It is believed that the first Christian settlement on this site was dedicated to a Celtic Bishop, Cyrillus (in Latin, Coriolanus) and was established *c*. 700. It is generally believed that the name, Killespickerill (Bishop Cyril's cell), derives from this source.

In the early thirteenth century John the Scot, Bishop of Dunkeld, whose see at that time included all the lands of Argyll, sent his chaplain, Harold, to Pope Innocent III with a plan to establish a new bishopric of Argyll. When the Pope approved the creation of the see of Argyll and established Harold as its first Bishop, the new prelate set up his cell at Killespickerill. (A second explanation for the strange name is Cill Easbuig Earailt – Bishop Harold's cell).

For more than thirty years Killespickerill was the headquarters of the see of Argyll. It was centrally positioned within reasonable distance of all the important settlements in Argyll. All the more reason then to wonder at the strange decision to establish the cathedral church on the Isle of Lismore during the thirteenth century.

The Minutes of the Synod of Argyll 1639–61 record that, 'In respect of the kirks of Gilespickerill and Ardchattan that were formerly united and served by one Minister as one cuire are now disunited by Committee for plantatione.' In 1605 the Commissioners ordained, 'the Kirks of Killespickerill and Ardchattan to be separate and served as two severall cuires in Time-coming'. They also ordained the stipend at, 'four chalder victual and three hundred score marks Scots money with forty marks for furnishing of communion yearly and one sufficient manse and Glebe'.

The ivy-covered ruins of the church of Killespickerill, dated 1228, still stand close to the present parish church of Muckairn which was built in 1829 and incorporates within its structure many of the stones from the earlier church. Churches, graveyard and manse all stand on a small elevation east of the hotel.

Tombstones of great antiquity were described by visitors to the burial ground in the nineteenth century, in particular those of the Sinclairs, one of the oldest families in the parish probably belonging to the fourteenth century. Other stones reported in 1880 as being of fifteenth-century origin have become buried although two of them have recently been uncovered again. Unfortunately their carvings are now all but obliterated. Here also is the burial place of Dr Dove MacCalman, who was born in Airds Bay. He founded the nineteenth-century Cottage Hospital in Oban which, as the West Highland Hospital, served the area of Lorn and the Isles until the opening of the new hospital at Soroba in 1995. Ludovic Grant, Master of the Lorn Furnace in the eighteenth century, is also buried here.

The village contains two further churches dating from the nineteenth century: the former Muckairn Free Church, which is now a private dwelling house, and the Church of the Visitation which was completed in 1902.

On a hillock which was partially removed in 1880 in order to accommodate the railway line, there once stood a stone cross of fourteenth- or fifteenth-century origin which has been likened to others at Kilbride near Lerags, south of Oban, and Kilberry in Knapdale. These crosses are associated with lands belonging to MacDonald, Lord of the Isles, and suggest an early connection with the Clan MacDonald which forfeited the title in 1462. The Taynuilt cross was shattered at some time early in the nineteenth century and its fragments were eventually recovered from the village dump by the Rev. Thomas MacKenzie, the Free Church minister at the time.

He presented the cross to the National Museums of Scotland. The hillock on which the cross stood still bears the name, Tom na Crois.

It is not known at exactly what date the village changed its name. The name Killespickerill is mentioned in several medieval documents relating to the area, a Campbell of Killespickerill having built the original Inverawe House. As well as appearing in the Minutes of the Synod of Argyll, 1639–1661 it is again mentioned in the 2cnd Statistical Account of 1840. There are records of the two parishes of Ardchattan and Muckairn being separated and co-joined on a number of occasions throughout their history but in 1829 Killispickerill was again given its own minister and has remained separate from Ardchattan ever since. The kirktoun of Muckairn is also mentioned in the archives but the name of Taynuilt derives from the later, droving and coaching days when the inn was known as the 'House by the Burn' or Tigh an Uillt.

From early in the seventeenth century until the first quarter of the twentieth century the lands surrounding Taynuilt were owned by the Campbells of Lochnell. They were eventually divided up into a number of smaller parcels of land. Today these are the estates of Muckairn, Airds Bay, comprising most of the village of Taynuilt, and Bonawe including the house and Home Farm. This estate originally included the Lorn Furnace.

On a hillock to the north of the parish church stands a pillar of rock, originally erected there by men from the Bonawe Furnace to commemorate one of Nelson's victories, most probably the Battle of the Nile. By the time the work was completed, however, Nelson was dead and so the intended inscription was changed to one in his memory. This claims to be the earliest of such memorials erected to the naval hero, anywhere in Britain. It bears the inscription:

TO THE MEMORY OF LORD NELSON THIS STONE WAS ERECTED BY THE
FURNACE WORKMEN 1805.

These fellows had a particular interest in the fight because it was they who had made the cannon balls used to sink the French fleet.

Today, in the midst of a wide plain spread out at the foot of the Cruachan mountain range, the village of Taynuilt stands upon a small rise above the level of the loch. The land is undulating glacial moraine, the soil suitable for both arable farming and the grazing of cattle and sheep. Once an area largely cultivated on the ancient crofting system, today there are several large farms grazing herds of cattle, sheep and in more recent times, deer to meet the growing demand for venison on the European markets. There are still a number of crofts within the village bounds and although most of these are now owner-occupied having substantial modern dwelling houses built upon them, their owners are still obliged to put the land to some kind of agricultural use. Horticulture, grazing or even tree planting are considered acceptable land usage.

As Taynuilt was the seat of the bishopric of Argyll in the sixth century it is probable that the village has had a school from that date. The earliest record of a school building, however, is of one maintained by the Society for the Promulgation of Christian Knowledge which was erected in 1734. This school had as many as thirty-eight pupils: twenty-two boys and sixteen girls. In the wall of the present school building, one section of which was erected in 1913, is a stone bearing the date 1834 which suggests a second school on the same site during the nineteenth century. What is certain is that schooling was provided for all the children in the parish long before it became compulsory.

The dominie for many years until his retirement in 1911, was a Mr Kenneth Beaton. A strict disciplinarian, he was not averse to using the tawse upon those pupils who would not or could not remember their lessons. It was a harsh way to gain his pupil's attention but it certainly worked for some children. A number of pupils from Taynuilt school, prior to the introduction of secondary education at Oban High School, were admitted straight into University at the age of fourteen. In 1990 Strathclyde Regional Council provided a new school building on a green-field site. The public school, built in 1895 and now abandoned, will, it is hoped, be utilised for public purposes or sold for private housing.

The village inn is of eighteenth-century origin but its gabled dormers and pedimented porch are of the early nineteenth century. Several rubble cottages of the same age survive, dotted around the village between much later structures. Their thatched roofs, clearly shown in nineteenth-century photographs, have been replaced with slate or corrugated iron. Many of the buildings lining the village street are of late Victorian or Edwardian date. The continued importance of Taynuilt as a centre for commerce in the parish is shown by the number of small businesses still trading despite competition from Oban and Glasgow, both within reasonable motoring distance.

Mr Robert MacLeod, who purchased the Airds Bay Estate from the Campbells in 1916, was a friend of John Logie Baird, one of the

Taynuilt village, *c.* 1880 (*Author's Collection*)

pioneers of television. In 1926 Robert took part in the earliest recorded television experiments when a crude image was transmitted from one room to another. Mr MacLeod was never happier than when in the company of children and young people. His name is synonymous in the village with the Christmas tree parties which he initiated and the Taynuilt Highland Games which attract visitors from all over the county.

Taynuilt village boasts a number of prestigious houses, mainly of Victorian origin. On the road through Glen Lonan, Barguillean House (now Lonan House), built in 1906–8 by the Macdonald family, was designed by Robert Lorimer, the famous Edinburgh architect. The house was turned into holiday flatlets late in the twentieth century. A second Lorimer-designed house, Ichrachan was built, *c.* 1908, a short distance to the south of the A85.

Before the Second World War, employment prospects in the village were limited to what jobs were available within the immediate area. When the iron foundry at Bonawe was operating many boys were apprenticed to the variety of trades employed there which included joinery and masonry as well as smelting and casting the iron. Apprenticeships were found in the services provided locally: gardening, retailing, in the blacksmith's forge and in road maintenance. Many village boys served their apprenticeship in paving-sett making at the Bonawe granite quarry on the north shore of Loch Etive. Others

Delivering the post, *c.* 1890 (*Author's Collection*)

worked on the land or joined the fishing fleets which operated out of every small coastal village. In addition the railway regularly employed local staff to operate the stations and maintain the track. When the Cruachan power station was constructed, 1950–65, it is estimated that at one time 2,000 men were employed in the various aspects of the job.

Except for those who were able to take up careers in teaching or nursing, girls inevitably went into service in the big houses and the villas of the middle classes. Some worked on the farms as dairy maids or as children's nannies. In the Second World War women were recruited to work on the land and in the munitions factories. Few returned to domestic service and many remained in the cities where they had gone to work. Today some school-leavers make a career on the land, in forestry or in fishing but others leave the district entirely after completing their schooling at Oban High School. A high proportion go on to Higher Education before finding employment.

Medical services are adequate for the village although there is no longer a resident doctor nearer than Connel. The District Nurse is the first port of call for those in trouble. Before the advent of telephones in every household, a lamp was flashed across the water from Bonawe Quarries on the north shore of Loch Etive when the nurse was required. In the days when there was a resident GP, his

Annual Outing of the Women's Temperance League (*Easdale Museum*)

practice covered a very wide area and included farms well off the beaten track, some of which could often be reached only on foot or horseback.

The village is a flourishing centre for every kind of social activity, many meetings taking place in the Public Hall which was built in 1905. Drama, music, and women's organisations share these premises together with youth groups such as Scouts and Guides and a number of sporting activities. Taynuilt boasts a flourishing horticultural society which has been in existence since 1928.

From Taynuilt the roads fan out to join the other villages in the parish.

Although the parishes of Ardchattan and Muckairn have been amalgamated and separated many times in the course of their history, no matter what ecclesiastical or political boundaries were drawn by those in Edinburgh or Westminster, the people intermingled freely, crossing Loch Etive by means of a ferry at the water's narrowest point to trade, to socialise, to work and to marry. So close are the two villages which unite the parishes that they bear the same name, Bonawe. On the north shore of the loch is the village of Bonawe Quarries and on the south shore, Bonawe itself which was the site of an important iron foundry for nearly 200 years.

The earliest building in Bonawe was an inn, a drovers' stance which stood close by the pier. This was soon joined by further buildings servicing the requirements of the passing trade. Strictly speaking therefore it owes its origin as a village to droving. Great changes were brought about in 1720, however, when the Loch Etive Trading Company leased rights from Lord Breadalbane to fell timber in Glen Kinglass on the western slopes of Ben Cruachan. In addition to producing vast quantities of charcoal, the company also traded in sawn timber for use in construction work and in tannin extracted from the bark of oak, birch and alder. A tannery built in Oban by the Stevenson brothers in the 1790s used bark for tannin from Bonawe.

In the beginning, charcoal manufactured here was exported to the regions in the north of England where iron ore was readily available. By 1725 however, it became clear that it was cheaper to bring the ore by sea to the source of timber rather than the other way around. Iron ore, haematite and limonite from Cumbria was imported and processed in the company's smelting plant which it had built at Kinglass on Loch Etive. The labour was recruited locally and the pig iron produced was shipped out by sea. In 1738 the Loch Etive Trading Company collapsed. The smelting plant at Kinglass was abandoned.

The seed had been sown, however, and, as with so many enterprises designed to develop industry in Argyll, it was the Duke in collaboration with the Earl of Breadalbane, who decided to try again. A Cumbrian iron foundry company, Newlands Ltd, was persuaded to lease land at Bonawe and build a new smelting plant. Ships of from 300–500 tons were employed to bring the ore from the south. Workers' dwellings were provided together with a church, school and a new quay, all of which remain today. As well as employing local labour, skilled and experienced workers were brought in from Cumbria, swelling the population in the parish and introducing new cultures into what had been a somewhat introspective community.

At the peak of its production, the Bonawe Furnace exported 700 tonnes of pig iron annually. This would have required charcoal from 3,500 tonnes of wood, derived from cutting down 30 hectares of woodland. Without careful husbandry the Argyll forests would soon have been laid waste as had been those of Cumbria and Northumberland.

The practice of coppicing ensured that stocks of timber were replaced quite rapidly. Trees such as birch and alder, ash and oak, when cut back carefully almost to the ground, sprout many branches where one trunk grew before. Over a period of years the trees became great bushes growing a thicket of sturdy green branches from their base. Thus the trees were retained in good health while yielding up all the timber required by the furnaces. The Lorn Furnace at Bonawe continued in operation until 1874. At the height of its prosperity it employed 600 men and a thriving village community grew up where once there had been only a ferry and a drovers' inn. The Newlands Company left its mark upon the district by building substantial roads for the transportation of timber and charcoal from the woodlands. Many of these are still in use today.

To ensure an efficient operation, the buildings servicing the furnaces were built into the contours of the landscape to make best use of the natural gravity afforded by the various slopes and hummocks. Water was drawn from the River Awe to drive an enormous water-wheel which powered the bellows used on the smelting floor.

During the Napoleonic Wars a large portion of the output from the Bonawe smelters went into the making of cannon balls. The story is told that at a time when it was thought that an invading French fleet might be on its way up the Firth of Lorn, the workers threw all their stocks of cannon balls into a great reservoir beside the manager's house to avoid their getting into enemy hands. These were never recovered and may well be resting on the floor of the pool to this day!

The buildings, which are in an excellent state of preservation, are now in the charge of the Department of the Environment. The workers' village consisted of two blocks of twenty typical industrial cottages built *c.* 1755 and a two-storey tenement block of the late eighteenth century together with an ironmaster's two-storey house. A number of smaller dwellings, intended for the woodcutters, also remain. Some houses have been modernised while other buildings – the church hall, bakery and laundry – have either fallen into disrepair or been used for different purposes. In the case of the Free Church, which was in use until 1857, much of the building's stone was removed to build up the banks of the River Nant.

So important was the foundry to the district that it had its own post office which remained open for long after the ironworks closed, continuing to handle mail for a wide area. The postmark for the district was 'Bunawe'.

A few local men continued producing small quantities of iron for a further twenty years but the majority were forced to find other work.

The tannery business also continued for some time, finally coming to an end shortly after the ironworks closed for good.

The only source of income now for the cottagers at Bonawe was that obtained by the women from their spinning and weaving. Crofting continued, together with fishing in both fresh waters and salt. Salmon and trout caught in the mountain burns, however, were the property of Lord Breadalbane and for some villagers poaching became a way of life. Cattle rearing, which had been the mainstay of the economy for centuries, continued.

The village of Kilchrenan which lies at the southern end of Glen Nant has had a long history. Conveniently situated beside Loch Awe it was the natural landing place for ferries from Portsonachan on the opposite shore. In the earliest times this was a route taken by pilgrims on their way to Iona and when cattle droving became important, there was a good stance here where herds might have to wait for days for a suitable ferry crossing.

It was in the village of Kilchrenan that the great Colin, founder of the Clan Campbell, fell in battle in 1294. A commemorative stone was placed in the churchyard by his descendant, the 8th Duke of Argyll, when Cairn Cailean, Colin's stone, was incorporated in the building of the new church in 1869.

In 1746 the York Building Company acquired various estates in western Scotland forfeited by Jacobite supporters after their defeat at Culloden. Both Glen Nant and Glen Avich were exploited for their exposures of building stone and a small hamlet was built near Kilchrenan to accommodate additional workers brought in from the north of England. This went by the name of New York until it was finally absorbed by the main village. Very good-quality limestone is still quarried a few miles north of Kilchrenan. Here an old limekiln was taken over in the 1950s by the Argyll Limestone Company and converted into a lime factory. Equipped with a modern stone crusher, the factory had an annual output of 6,000 tons of lime in the early 1960s.

Before its amalgamation with Muckairn the parish church of Kentallen was that at Kilchrenan. A second church was erected at Dalavich in 1771 and at Portsonachan on the further shore of the loch but still within the parish, stands another of the prefabricated tin churches like the Cathedral in Oban, erected in the nineteenth century.

In such a widespread parish the siting of a manse presented immense difficulty. The minister's house was eventually built overlooking Loch Awe, two miles from Kilchrenan and eight from Dalavich.

In the most ancient part of Kilchrenan churchyard are medieval monuments carved in the style of the Loch Awe School. Of more recent date is the monument of an army surgeon, Robert MacIntyre, who on his death in 1815 bequeathed considerable sums of money for public purposes in the parish.

The Glen Nant woodlands lie in a well-sheltered valley which enjoys the mild climate of the western seaboard without suffering from the prevailing winds. One of the few areas of forest left in Scotland whose deciduous trees have not been ousted by faster growing softwoods, it has a unique flora including many hundreds of different species of mosses, liverworts and lichens, some of which are very rare. Dyeing fabrics using the lichens, heather and bark of trees to be found in Glen Nant, was a craft exercised by the women of the district for many centuries. Glen Nant was also a famous haunt of illicit whisky distillers and the tale is told of a tailor who is said to have been distilling whisky when the Excise men arrived to arrest him. Leading them away from his hidden still, the tailor ran off with the Excise men in pursuit. Coming to the river, halfway up the glen, he was forced to take a mighty leap in order to clear a forty-foot-high waterfall. He evaded capture and his feat is recorded for posterity on Ordnance Survey maps of the area where it is shown as the Tailor's Leap (Leum na Tailleir).

As part of a scheme to supply water to the surrounding area, Glen Nant was partially submerged during the building of the Glen Nant dam. A considerable amount of woodland was lost. In recent years the true value of the area has been appreciated and what woodland remains has been preserved for the nation as an area of special scientific interest.

The parish, which as a whole was unsuitable for grazing sheep, was unaffected by clearances of the nineteenth century, nevertheless the population had been seriously depleted by the 1900s. Two world wars were later responsible for the loss of population. One and a half thousand parishioners in 1881 had been reduced to 349 by 1951.

In 1928 the Forestry Commission became a major employer in the parish when it began a scheme for replanting denuded woodlands. By the 1950s a new village had been built alongside the already existing village of Dalavich on the shores of Loch Awe.

Forestry Commision village at Dalavich (*Author's Collection*)

The present church, *c.* 1771, was built by the Sonachan Campbells who had their own burial enclosure constructed in 1779, but the burial ground suggests a Christian settlement of greater antiquity for it contains several medieval gravestones carved in the style of the Loch Awe School. Amongst the more recent memorials is that of John McPherson, schoolmaster at Ardchonnel, who died in 1902. Ardchonnel school served a scattered population and was used for church services on occasion but until the mid-twentieth century the settlement had never developed beyond a drovers' stance. The Forestry Commision provided a new school and community hall and water and electrical supplies were installed for the benefit of all the villagers. Although the Commission long ago sold off its houses to individual purchasers, it continued to provide these services. In the 1980s however, the Hydro Board took over the electrical supply and in 2002 the Commission sold its remaining holdings to a developer proposing to build a holiday complex close to the village. Existing residents protested loudly when they found that no arrangement had been made to continue to supply them with water from the estate. They were incensed too when they discovered that the new owner intended to use the village hall for the exclusive use of his own clients. Built by the Commission for the enjoyment of all the residents, the hall had always been the focal point of village life. The legal wrangling continues over parts of the village which are thought to have been in common ownership. This is unfortunately a typical outcome of the legacy left by a feudal form of land ownership which still exists in some parts of the Highlands.

With improved communications and travel there is now a steady movement of people into this area of the county. Affordable housing in both Kilchrenan and Dalavich is again in great demand.

Perhaps the saddest loss to the community in the past one hundred years has been that of craftsmen once employed locally. In 1900 the area boasted 40 woodcutters and dykers, 22 weavers, 6 shoemakers, 6 tailors and 4 millers. By 1960 there remained one building contractor employing 2 men. More recently the advent of tourism has encouraged the return to the area of artists and craftsmen of various kinds, woodworkers, painters and potters. Despite the advent of television, there is still a call for public entertainment in these isolated communities and this is provided by travelling film shows and theatrical performances given in the village halls.

The village of Lochawe owes its existence to its position near the head of the loch where its western arm breaks away from the main waters to drain northwards via the River Awe into Loch Etive and the sea. The heavily wooded island of Innis Chonain (St Conan's Isle) lies a few yards off-shore, attached now to the mainland by a narrow causeway. This must have been an attractive site for early settlement and is supposed to be the burial place of St Conan who arrived here in the middle of the sixth century to set up his cell at Dalmally.

In the nineteenth century, the island became the home of the Campbells of Blytheswood who built the existing mansion. In 1881 Walter Douglas Campbell of Blytheswood began the building of St Conan's Kirk in Lochawe village. It started as a simple chapel for the benefit of the local people and was opened for worship in 1886. Walter Campbell was a collector of antiquities and, determined to provide a suitable place in which to display his treasures, he now set out to extend the church. The work was not completed until 1930, some years after his death.

It is a strange building, leaving one uncertain whether it is meant to be a folly or a place of worship. At first sight it would appear to be a medieval building to which has been added a nineteenth-century church. In fact, the opposite is the truth for later additions to the building have been made to emulate every aspect of Scottish architecture through the ages. One enters by way of a stone-built

St Conan's Kirk, Lochawe, designed by Walter Douglas Campbell (*Author's Collection*)

cloister reminiscent of that at Iona. The church itself, however, is pure nineteenth-century Gothic architecture with a few Norman-style pillars and a crypt thrown in for good measure. The only ancient things about the building are the granite from which it is constructed, hewn from the mountain towering over it, and a number of artefacts gathered from places of worship around the country. If, anticipating an ancient monument, one can overcome the initial sensation of having been cheated, the unusual nature of St Conan's Kirk and its interesting collection of ecclesiastical treasures must compensate for the disappointment!

Houses varying in age from late nineteenth-century to modern, an inn and a village shop are strung out alongside the main road, occupying a narrow strip of land at the foot of Ben Cruachan and separating it from the waters of the loch. The towers and turrets of hotels, built in the 1880s, are witness to the efforts of the Earl of Breadalbane to cash in on the rising interest in tourism. In 1882, he introduced steamers to the loch providing sightseeing trips as well as a regular passenger service for those wishing to travel between Ford and Dalmally. The first steamer, *Countess of Breadalbane*, was 99 ft in

St Conan's Kirk: cloister (*Author's Collection*)

length and 14 ft across the beam. She carried one hundred passengers and in the early days, the Dalmally Hotel which was also owned by the Earl of Breadalbane operated a service which combined a stay at the hotel with a trip around the loch. By 1890 there were three public and five or six privately owned vessels offering trips on Loch Awe. For fifty years during the twentieth century there were no pleasure boats at all on the loch but in the 1980s one of the old steam boats was reintroduced and still offers cruises during the summer season.

The railway arrived here in 1880. A station in its original form serves the village and a pair of railway workers' cottages still clings to the water's edge beside the line.

To the west of Lochawe village the loch divides into two main waterways, the right-hand fork culminating in the River Awe which drains into Loch Etive to the north. Following the last Ice Age, the river has cut a deep gorge between the rocks to form the Pass of Brander. Here the mountainside falls almost vertically to the bank of the river leaving scarcely sufficient room even for a road. In the 1880s the railway track had to be blasted out of the mountainside at a higher level.

River Awe and the Pass of Brander (*Author's Collection*)

The Cruachan mountain range of seven peaks, four miles in length and standing at over 1,000 metres at its highest point, forms one of the most splendid of Scotland's mountains. A barrier to the incoming winds from the Atlantic, it has an exceptionally high annual rainfall and creates a huge watershed for the surrounding lands. The Celts had many stories to explain natural phenomena encountered in their everyday lives. The creation of Loch Awe was one of these:

> Beithir, the winter hag or Cailleach is the embodiment of darkness, cold and death. She created thunder and lightening to roar and crackle in the hills and let loose the dreaded storm wolves or Faoilteach, to howl across the black waters of the Firth of Lorn and down Loch Etive. Beithir was not always a hag however. Once she was beautiful, maintaining her good looks by bathing every day in the waters of a spring which arose from the upper slopes of Ben Cruachan. The Gods granted this concession on condition that Beithir covered the spring with a great stone, each evening at sundown, to conserve the waters within the mountain. During the day Beithir tended her sheep and cattle on the lower slopes of the Ben. One day, seeking to relieve the boredom of her lonely life, she drove her stock to new pastures on the fertile plains of the island of Mull. The cattle too enjoyed the change, wandering great distances and causing their mistress to spend a long time collecting them up for the journey home.

Beithir arrived just as the sun was going down, so tired that she fell asleep before covering the spring. The waters cascaded down the mountainside throughout the night until the voices of children were silenced in the glen and the lowing of cattle could no longer be heard. By morning when she awoke, the valley was flooded and Loch Awe stretched for twenty miles towards the sea. The Gods sealed the spring forever, imprisoning Beithir beneath the stone. Unable to bathe in the waters, she quickly lost her looks and became the ugly and malicious Hag who causes dark clouds to hang above the mountain top and thunder to roar between the hills.

Today the Pass of Brander is famous as the location for the largest hydroelectricity generating plant in Scotland. The operation which began in the 1960s was designed to ensure that, despite the huge scale of the installation, it would not impinge upon the landscape in any way. The only outward evidence of its existence is the massive dam which was built high up the mountain to retain water for use in generating power. All other aspects of the operation are hidden within the mountain itself where vast underground caverns house turbines and generators, men and machines which at peak times contribute up to 400,000 kW of electricity, a quarter of all Scotland's electrical output to the National Grid. In its efficiency of operation the Cruachan scheme is second to none in Great Britain. It employs a large number of well-qualified engineers and technicians bringing much-needed high-grade employment to the county of Argyll. Following the installation of the Cruachan Power Station, mains electricity was, by the 1970s, made available to even the most remote areas in the county.

The main obstacle to travel through the Pass of Brander was the River Awe itself which had to be crossed in order to reach Dalmally. After a period of continuous rain or at the spring melt when the river was in spate, drovers, troops and pilgrims were obliged to wait on the bank until the river could be forded. A three–arched stone bridge was constructed in 1779 by Captain William Pitman. In addition to a grant from the Commission for Forfeited Estates (a fund accrued as a result of the 1745 Rising) subscriptions were raised from Breadalbane, the Duke of Argyll and others to pay the cost of construction in the region of £1,000.

The Bridge of Awe was built from stone quarried at the site. This coarse-textured sandstone formed the outer leaves of the bridge, the centre being infilled with rubble. The bridge was wide enough and strong enough to carry traffic of the nineteenth and early twentieth centuries but by the 1930s it had become clear that it must either be enlarged or replaced. The decision was made to reroute the main highway, the A85, so that it crossed the river a few hundred yards to the north and a new bridge was completed in 1938. The old bridge continued in use for foot and horse traffic until the centre arch was washed away in a flash flood in the 1990s.

The original drovers' road from north Argyll made a crossing of Loch Etive from the location of the present Bonawe Quarries on the north shore to the village of Inverawe at the mouth of the River Awe. The *Penny Ferry* carried passengers and beasts across the loch.

For several hundred years the village was the stronghold of the Clan Campbell. Despite the fact that in the *Commons of Argyll* of 1692 twenty-seven properties controlled by the Campbells are listed, they still regard this as their home and the clan's rallying cry even today, is *CRUACHAN*!

There has been building of one kind or another on this site for centuries: earthworks, medieval castle and fortified house have succeeded one another down the ages. Today's Inverawe House is a modest dwelling by comparison with its predecessors. It has a central tower which may be medieval in origin but has been much altered over the centuries. A three-bay extension at the north end is of eighteenth-century construction and there is evidence of the remodelling work carried out in the 1850s by Charles Wilson in the crowsteps and baronial turrets. Today the house is of two storeys, the walls harled and painted white under a slated roof with dormers and blackened crowsteps and window surrounds.

There are many ghostly tales and stories of treachery associated with the place, one of which concerned a plot to kill the young heir to the Chieftainship of the clan. The young Campbell, surrounded by a small body of his supporters and with his great hunting dog running along at his side, arrived at Inverawe to claim his inheritance from his uncle who had been acting as his steward while he was a minor. The jealous, self-seeking, uncle was reluctant to hand over control when the time came and planned to assassinate the boy. Feigning allegiance to his nephew, the uncle invited the lad to take his seat at the head of the banqueting table. Before he could do so, however, the hungry hound, anxious to get at the food, leapt onto his master's chair which collapsed under him revealing the nest of knives below. Arranged to destroy the young laird, the trap killed his dog instead. The young laird retreated with his retinue, returning later with a force strong enough to take Inverawe Castle by force.

One evening in the mid-eighteenth century, the Laird of Inverawe, Duncan Campbell, was disturbed by a loud knocking on his door. Outside he found a fellow, breathless from running, his clothing torn and smeared with blood. The stranger begged for asylum saying that he had killed a man and that his pursuers were even then upon his heels. As Duncan Campbell led the man to a secret hiding place within the castle his visitor turned on him demanding he swear an oath not to betray him. 'Swear on your dirk!' demanded the stranger and Duncan swore. Soon a party of Campbell's own kinsmen came knocking at the door crying, 'Your cousin Donald has been murdered and we are seeking his killer.' Duncan Campbell, bound by his oath, could say nothing of the fugitive and the men went on their way.

As he lay sleeping that night Campbell was visited by the ghost of his dead relative who stood beside his bed and in deep sepulchral tones declared 'Inverawe . . . Inverawe, blood has been shed. Shield not the murderer.'

Next morning the Laird went to his guest and demanded he leave the house. When the man protested Duncan compromised by leading him to a cave on the hillside where he would be safe from his pursuers.

The next night the ghost came again. Clearly dissatisfied with what Duncan had done he cried, 'Farewell Inverawe . . . until we meet again at Ticonderoga!'

The name meant nothing to Campbell but he was to recall the incident vividly when, while serving as a major with the Black Watch, in the American War of Independence, he was called upon to attack a fort called Ticonderoga. The night before the attack he was again visited by the ghost and next morning told his comrades, 'I shall die today.' His prophecy was fulfilled.

At the Penny Ferry landing there was an old inn called the Tigh na h-Aibhne which still existed within living memory. This was an old drovers' inn beside which stood the house of the ferryman. The inn was demolished to make way for the development of Inverawe Power Station in the 1960s but the ruins of the ferryman's house remain.

The inn figures in the journals of many famous travellers. It was here that McIan of Glencoe rested in December 1691 on his journey to take that fateful oath of allegiance at Inverary. In his account of a journey through Argyll in 1769, Thomas Pennant describes not only the ironworks but also a large salmon hatchery at the mouth of the River Awe. There is a trout farm and hatchery there today. Describing a visit she made with her brother in 1803 Dorothy Wordsworth recalls her pleasure at finding the inn here so comfortable and the landlady so obliging:

> We had an excellent supper – fresh salmon, a fowl, gooseberries and cream and potatoes; good beds; and the next morning boiled milk and bread and were charged only seven shillings and sixpence for the whole . . . horse, liquor, supper and the two breakfasts. We thought they had made a mistake and told them so for it was only half as much as we paid the day before at Dalmally, the case being that Dalmally is in the main road of the tourists.

Travelling further eastward from Inverawe, a string of tiny hamlets including Inverleiver, Ardmaddy and Ardkinglas occupy the eastern shore of Loch Etive. There settlements relate to the time when Glen Kinglass was exploited for its timber and later an iron-smelting plant was set up there. Charcoal burners and woodsmen lived in these remote villages, which until fairly recently were accessible only by water. Today all but a few dwellings have been abandoned. Those remaining house families working for various estates in the area. Children even today still have a considerable journey on foot or in their parent's vehicles before reaching the school bus pick-up point.

With its growing permanent population and with loyal support from outreach villages in the parish, there is reason to hope that the district as a whole will grow and prosper with emphasis not only upon tourism but also upon the numerous small enterprises which make this such an interesting and vibrant community.

7
BARCALDINE AND BENDERLOCH

*Paving stones for the streets of Glasgow
and the magical properties of seaweed*

The north shore of Loch Etive at the point where the loch enters the Sound of Lorn was first settled around 7,000 years ago. The flat coastal area offered land suitable for cultivation, while the higher ground which rises sharply to the east and north made the area relatively easy to defend. Both fresh- and salt-water fishing and forests full of game provided for the needs of a large community.

To the north and east of the old Connel ferry and the present-day bridge lies an extensive area of boggy ground with several small lochans. This bears the romantic name of the Moss of Achnacree. The perimeter of this ancient bog holds well-preserved evidence of the earliest men to settle in the region. Neolithic cairns from the Stone Age (*c.* 3000 BC) and cists and barrows of the Iron Age (1000 BC–AD 200) have been discovered here while a little to the north, at Benderloch, are to be found cup-and-ring markings of the Bronze Age (*c.* 1500 BC) and standing stones also of great antiquity.

The discovery of foundations of a considerable settlement, with evidence of stone-walled buildings and flagged floors, has given considerable cause for argument and speculation by archaeologists and historians for many centuries. Dated two to three centuries BC, Dun Mac Sniachan is a Celtic fortification situated to the west of the Oban to Fort William road, on a ridge close by the shore of Ardmucknish Bay. Thomas Pennant in his *Voyages to the Hebrides* of 1772, mentions the site in his description of his crossing of the mouth of Loch Etive: 'Crossed the ferry at Connel. A mile from Connel near the north shore is Dun-mac-Uisneachain [the fort of the sons of Uisneach], the ancient city of Beregonium.'

Pennant was quoting from an apocryphal account of the origins of these remains. The site had for long been regarded by scholars as that of the city of Beregonium, described by Ptolemy in his *Geography of the World*, although there was nothing in either local tradition or place-names to suggest that a settlement of this name ever existed there.

Pennant suggests that the settlement, which he attributes to Fergus II, was for many generations the chief city in Scotland. The district was undoubtedly important in Scotland's early history. Several Scottish kings were crowned at Dunstaffnage before the Coronation Stone was removed to Scone in Perthshire.

Early in the nineteenth century, archaeologists, inspired by Pennant's account, flocked to the area and enthusiastically, if imaginatively, identified watercourses, columns and paved streets which they related to pre- and post-Roman occupation. Claudius Ptolemaeus (Ptolemy), geographer and astronomer, worked in Alexandria during the middle years of the first century AD and the information for his *Geography* came from the observations of those Romans he met who had visited Britain. There is, however, no evidence to link the Roman invaders with Loch Etive. It is, in fact, doubtful if they ever reached this far north. Subsequent investigations have placed the site of Ptolemy's city of Beregonium much further south, in Galloway.

From Pennant's 1772 description there appears to have been a fortified town sited within thick woodland and surrounded by ramparts and a fosse or dry moat. It was clearly a place of retreat from invaders. Running along the top of the beach there was a raised mound possibly used as a lookout point as well as a defensive emplacement.

The name ascribed by Pennant, Dun Mac Uisneach, relates to the ancient story of Deirdre and her lover who took refuge here from Deirdre's guardian Conchobar, King of Ulster. Conchobar, planning to marry Deirdre himself when she came of age, had his infant ward removed to a place of seclusion. In due course she met and fell in love with Naoise, a handsome young member of the House of Uisneach. Fearing the wrath of her guardian, Deirdre, Naoise and two of his brothers fled across the sea to Alba and took refuge on the shores of Loch Etive. Conchobar, determined to retrieve his ward, sent a messenger with greetings to the brothers, inviting them to return to Ulster with Deirdre and all would be forgiven. Deirdre did not trust her uncle but the young men, homesick for Ireland, accepted the invitation and returned, only to be imprisoned and executed. Deirdre, in despair, plunged a dagger into her heart and toppled into the grave with her lover and his brothers. The tribal war which resulted from Conchobar's deception resulted in bitter fighting between the two houses. Conchobar was finally defeated and the House of Ulster was destroyed, thereby fulfilling an ancient prophecy that the House of Ulster would be brought down by the sons of Uisneach.

Ardchattan Priory (*Author's Collection*)

On the north shore of Loch Etive stands the ancient priory and village of Ardchattan. Founded in 1230 by Duncan MacDougall, Lord of Lorne, the priory was one of three houses of the Valliscaulian Order(of Benedictine observance) established in Scotland at that time. Dedicated to St Mary and St John the Baptist, the priory's endowments included lands and rights in Benderloch and Appin but also tiends of the churches of Baile Mhaodain, Kilninver and Kilbrandon in Netherlorn.

The life of the thirty monks installed here was austere, requiring absolute silence, prayers seven times in every twenty-four hours, the wearing of hair shirts and sleeping fully clothed. There was complete abstinence from meat.

Following his victory over John MacDougall of Lorne, King Robert the Bruce held a royal council at the priory in 1308. Apart from the names of some of the earlier priors and a number of tombstones in the churchyard at Ardchattan, there is little recorded history of the priory before 1500. In 1508, Duncan MacArthur was promoted to the office of Prior by King James IV. He is attributed with having restored the then ruinous church and other buildings and being responsible for reviving the religious life of the community by appointing the six religious brothers the priory was able to support. A section of wall from this period of reconstruction remains. In 1565 the leading cleric of the Reformed Church, John Carswell, adopted the title of Bishop of the Isles which today is assigned to the leading Roman Catholic prelate of Argyll. His grave is believed to be close to the west wall of the priory. In the middle of the sixteenth century John Campbell, a younger son of Campbell of Cawdor, was appointed Commendator and Prior of Ardchattan. Although monastic religious life as such ceased with the Reformation, following the Dissolution and the death of the last monk King James VI granted Campbell all rights and titles associated with the Priory and he took the title Laird of Ardchattan. John continued to reside there until his death in 1602 when he was succeeded by his son, Alexander. The property has to this day remained in the hands of the same family.

The refectory buildings became the Commendator's house and the choir and transepts were converted for services of the Reformed Church. Two burial aisles were added at this time.

Although the medieval church has long been a ruin and many of its stones removed for other buildings, there is clear indication of a building of cruciform plan. There were extensions made to the chancel in the late sixteenth and early seventeenth century.

Despite the difficulties experienced by Catholic families after the Reformation, the Campbells of Ardchattan remained loyal to their chosen confession and supported any and every movement to restore the country to the Roman Catholic faith. John Campbell, 2nd Laird of Ardchattan, supported the Royalist cause during the Civil War. In 1644 he is said to have assisted Colkitto's army to cross Loch Etive via the Connel ferry on condition that his own lands would not be burnt. Between 1653 and 1654 Campbell garrisoned Ardchattan on behalf of Charles II, whereupon Cromwell's Governor of Dunstaffnage, Captain Mutloe, raided the house, taking prisoners, weapons and ammunition. The laird later claimed that the house had been ransacked and burnt, this is thought to have been an exaggeration made in the hope of gaining compensation for the damage.

Although by this time the Priory's associated buildings had been appropriated for domestic use, part of the old monastic church was still in use for parochial worship. In 1678 it was reported that the fabric of the church was in ruins and no longer suitable for public worship. No doubt some renovations were carried out nevertheless, for it was a century and a half later that a new parish church was finally erected on a fresh site.

At some time in the intervening period, the Campbells decided to erect a church to serve the communities of both Benderloch and Ardchattan and, hoping to avoid accusations of favouring one village over the other, erected one halfway between the two settlements. To the chagrin of all the worshippers, the church of Baile Mhaodain necessitated a walk of several miles from either village in order to attend church services several times a week and twice on Sundays.

In 1836 the present Ardchattan Parish Church was built. The church building undoubtedly incorporated some of the masonry from the dismantled choir of the old monastery. Other stonework was appropriated for use in building the adjacent mansion so that by 1798 there were complaints that the possessor of the property had destroyed the old priory for the sake of a few stones. Having abandoned the old conventual buildings which they had occupied since the dissolution of the priory, the Ardchattan Campbells now resided in the fine new mansion house, next door. In 1815 an Oban builder, John Drummond, carried out repairs to this and between 1847 and 1855 substantial alterations were made under the direction of the Glasgow Architect, Charles Wilson. The house retains its Jacobean character but in extending over the foundations of the former cloister and nave Wilson incorporated a small vaulted pulpit room opening through a pointed arch arcade from the east end of the old refectory.

The remaining portion of the choir and transepts of the monastic church came into the guardianship of the Department of the Environment in 1954.

The village of Bonawe Quarries, situated a few kilometres to the east of Ardchattan, has had a mixed history. Having begun as a drovers' stance it was to become an important source of building stone. From medieval times the Breadalbane Campbells had worked a quarry here, shipping their building requirements out by sea. When the original quarry was worked out, excavations moved from Craig Point to the present position close to the ferry landing.

As the cities of Glasgow and Edinburgh grew, Bonawe granite setts were in great demand for paving the streets. In the twentieth century both the entrance to the Mersey Tunnel and the King George V Bridge in Glasgow were constructed of Bonawe granite blocks. Such was the importance of the quarry during the nineteenth century that a two-storey tenement block, reminiscent of those of the same date found in Glasgow, was built to accommodate more than sixty quarry workers and their families. The quarry was purchased in 1892 by J. & A. Gardner who also worked the slate quarries at Ballachulish and owned their own steamship for transporting materials to the cities of the south. A hundred years on, the same company still owns the site although the quarrying rights are leased elsewhere.

The speed at which this village grew from nothing more than a drover's stance and a few cottages is a measure of the importance of stone as a building material in the late nineteenth century. There is no mention at all of a village at Bonawe Quarries in the census return of 1861, the only houses listed being those of the ferryman and the blacksmith. Both of these were situated on the tiny island called Duirniss which lies a few meters offshore in Loch Etive.

In 1871 the census return listed a further nine houses. These were known as the Bonawe Quarries Cottages. One house was occupied by the quarry manager and his family, the others by quarry workers and the store-keeper. From the start, the company provided a store where the workers were obliged to obtain all their requirements, often being charged inflated prices. With housing provided by the company and universal indebtedness to the company store, the workforce was virtually bound to the company's service. It made for a very stable workforce but led to a great deal of heartache. Early in the twentieth century, the trade unions fought for and eventually achieved the abolition of company stores throughout Britain. It appears that the amount of accommodation provided was still insufficient for the men working at Bonawe Quarries for in 1871 five of the workers' dwellings listed one or more lodgers in addition to family members. The remainder of the workforce at that time must have been drawn from Taynuilt and the villages of Bonawe and Inverawe across the water. Two more cottages appear to have been built at this period close to the original quarry at Craig Point. In these lived a total of eleven people.

By 1881 the original quarry workers' cottages had been replaced by a series of houses occupied by approximately 200 people including women and children. Many of the inhabitants were single men who lodged in a boarding house run by a housekeeper and her daughter. Further houses were added early in the twentieth century and at some later date the older, 1880s, buildings were demolished. By 1900 the quarry employed 300 men and to accommodate the additional numbers some prefabricated corrugated-iron houses lined in timber were erected in various spots around the village. None of these houses had piped water or drainage, all water being drawn from a standpipe at the end of the village street. Coal was delivered to the quay from boats returning from Glasgow having delivered their load of building stone.

In 1910 two more tenement blocks were erected which became known as the Ferry Island Buildings and the Gullet Buildings. Of these only the Ferry Island Buildings remain today in a ruinous condition. Between 1900 and 1910 the narrow strait between the island and the shore was infilled with quarry waste to make a firm road across to the ferry landing.

In 1914 the village of Bonawe Quarries had a population of over 1,000 people, every house being crammed full with families and their lodgers. With the growth of population in the village, amenities steadily improved. A village hall was built about 1910. The people provided their own musical entertainment and dances; weddings and other special events were well attended. By this time, the village of Bonawe Quarries had its own post office, a small corrugated-iron hut situated opposite the village stores. Milk was delivered daily from a local farm. Arriving in churns, it would be distributed straight into the housewives' jugs as they gathered around the cart in the village street.

The workforce increased rapidly during the General Strike of 1926 when a great many miners arrived from the Lanarkshire coalfields seeking employment. With such an influx of labour the quarrymaster could now pick and choose whom he employed and wages might be lowered without fear of loss of output. This was a time of great anxiety and considerable strife creating wounds which were long in the healing. Most of the miners returned to their former employment when the strike ended but others remained in Argyll, blending with the community and establishing family connections which exist to this day.

In the 1930s, travelling shops arrived in the form of motorised vehicles. These included a bakery, a fishmonger who also sold fruit and vegetables, and a butcher. The Oban Co-Operative store delivered weekly. The village never had a church of its own, those at Ardchattan and Taynuilt being within fairly easy travelling distance of the village.

With the outbreak of war in 1939 many of the younger men left the quarries to join the fighting services and their families were obliged to move out. The vacated houses, particularly the corrugated-iron constructions built at the turn of the century, were quickly taken up by families evacuated from the cities. The evacuees paid rent to the quarrying company and when the war was over several families retained their leases or purchased the houses for use as holiday cottages. Apart from a small group of new bungalows built in 1948 for senior members of the quarry staff, there was no further development within the village.

The demand for granite setts for road-building had ended before the war and brick construction, cheaper than stone block, was being employed in rebuilding the cities devastated by bombing. To keep the men in some sort of employment, the company constructed a tar-making plant on the site but this was only to ward off the evil day when many of them were eventually laid off.

In 1965 Argyll County Council provided a new development of twenty-six corporation houses in an attempt to improve rural housing stock. These new homes were equipped with all modern conveniences and despite the fact that it meant moving to the outskirts of the village, many of those remaining in the substandard accommodation provided by the company housing were only too pleased to go. Only elderly people now lived in the village, most of them on Ferry Island. The majority of the old houses were demolished and only the shell of the apartment block remains as a reminder of the period of greatest productivity in the quarry.

By 2000 the quarry was again in full production, mechanisation having replaced all but a few of the workforce once employed. High-grade road stone and granite blocks for more prestigious building are exported in large quantity to all parts of the UK and the Continent of Europe. Unfortunately it is no longer possible to remove the quarried stone by sea. Large lorries travel daily between Bonawe Quarries and markets in the south. The renewed activity has met with considerable dissension from the local residents who have, not without justification, consistently voiced their objections to the use of very large vehicles on the inadequate, extremely narrow access road. Like Easdale and other places in Argyll, Bonawe Quarries is an example of a single industry creating an entire community and, at its own demise, destroying it. While other settlements in Argyll can boast a history going back for centuries, this village lasted little more than sixty years.

To the west of Connel Bridge stands the village of North Connel. This is a small community of commuters who enjoy the feeling of remoteness, which the South Shian Peninsula offers, as well as the convenience of easy access to Oban. Most of the houses date from the mid-twentieth century although the Lochnell Arms Hotel was almost certainly built on or near the site of an original drovers' stance. The village's greatest claim to fame is the presence of a small airfield which was established by the Royal Air Force during the Second World War. Connel Airfield has become a popular venue for civilian pilot training and for pleasure and private business flights. Discussions continue with the aim of establishing a civil air terminal for direct flights to and from the cities and to link up with passing traffic bound for the islands.

Today Benderloch is the main village in the parish although historically the lands lying between Loch Etive and Loch Creran all came under the name of Barcaldine. Benderloch is approached from the Connel Bridge along the Fort William road, which skirts the shore of Loch Linnhe. It appears at first sight to be a twentieth-century settlement. Houses and shops of indifferent architecture straddle the road in the haphazard manner of ribbon development in the 1930s. The early nineteenth-century school and schoolhouse stand outwith the present village at the township of Ledaig, Lochnell school, in the centre of the village, having replaced it in the 1980s. The former United Free Church built in 1911 is now a private house. In the village centre is St Modan's Church, which was built in 1904.

The impression that the village has grown up around the tourism industry is confirmed, it seems, by the appearance of a very large caravan site close beside the road. In order to explore the real history of the village it is necessary to take one of the side roads where historic houses and their estates give a clearer picture of how the villages of Benderloch, and to the north, Barcaldine, developed.

To the west of the village is a group of ancient crofts, their cottages largely reconstructed by Argyll County Council to an acceptable standard during the 1950s, formerly in the feu of the great landowners who, from the thirteenth century to the nineteenth, were the Breadalbane Campbells.

The first recorded major landowner was Sir Colin Campbell of Glenorchy who in 1470 received from his nephew, Colin Campbell, the 1st Duke of Argyll, 'six merklands of Barcaldine'. There is no doubt that the site upon which Barcaldine Castle stands has been in use as a stronghold ever since. The present Barcaldine Castle, however, dates only from 1601 when Sir Duncan Campbell of Glenorchy ordered his kinsman, Alexander Campbell, who had restored Kilchurn, to restore the existing castle at Barcaldine. The result of this reconstruction was the castle as it is today. It consists of a simple L-shaped tower house with a round stair-tower set in the angle which also acts as the entrance to the castle. The walls are harled with small, randomly spaced openings. The three gables are crowstepped and at each corner a corbelled round tower is, like the stair tower, topped off with a conical capping of slate. When the work of reconstruction was well under way, Duncan Campbell conferred upon Alexander the Captaincy of the castle. Unfortunately, this honour was accompanied by the requirement to keep the building in good order, all repairs to be paid for by the incumbent!

Over the centuries the castle has remained in the hands of the Campbells. With long periods of neglect in between, it has from time to time been renovated and is now a comfortable family home.

Alexander Campbell took the title Campbell of Lochnell, from his own family home in Lorn. In 1671, he left the castle in the hands of a kinsman and moved into Lochnell House.

This house, which Alexander had built on the shores of Ardmucknish Bay, was of two storeys, simple and dignified like many farmhouses of the period. In 1737–9 John Douglas was commissioned to build a three-storey Georgian mansion alongside, the old house being used as the service area for the new. In 1816 an L-plan block united its predecessors, overpowering their simple dignity with a five-bay front and other over-elaborate decoration including a pedimented centrepiece carrying classical urns and the castellations so favoured by the Victorians. This house remained in Campbell possession until 1918 when it was sold to the Earl of Dundonald.

Around 1768 a house was commissioned by John Campbell of Barcaldine at the head of Loch Creran. Built by the mason John Menelaws of Greenock, this building, much restored and extended, was for some years a country house hotel, but is now once again a private dwelling house.

Barcaldine House became the family home of the Barcaldine Campbells in 1724 when James Duff, mason of Oban, was commissioned by Patrick Campbell to erect a fine dwelling house at a spot some six kilometres to the east of Barcaldine Castle. A few years later

Barcaldine Castle (*copyright © RCAHMS*)

Duff was again engaged to add a kitchen and in 1759 an additional storey converted the house into the present three-storey structure. In 1815 a court of offices designed by James Gillespie Graham was added together with, in 1831, a Jacobean-style library. A wing providing additional bedrooms appeared in 1838. The resulting structure is a rambling building whose best feature is the well-designed garden ground in which it stands.

On the Isle of Eriska, lying off the north-west tip of the South Shian Peninsula in a secluded setting, a large family house was built by Hippolyte Blanc in 1884. This towered and castellated baronial style mansion lent itself readily to conversion to a hotel in the latter part of the twentieth century.

Apart from the castle and other great houses associated with the village of Benderloch, one of the oldest buildings in the district is the schoolhouse at Ferlochan, a couple of kilometres to the east of Barcaldine Castle. This is a long, single-storey building once thatched in heather but now slated. The schoolhouse was one of a number erected in the Ardchattan parish early in the nineteenth century.

Employment in the area was, until very recently, restricted mainly to agriculture, crofting and fishing. In the *Third Statistical Account of Scotland* (1961), Mrs Mary Campbell-Preston of Ardchattan records that her earliest memories were of summer evenings when the lochs would be alive with small boats fishing for whiting and 'cuddies' (young coalfish). By 1961 there was little fishing on the lochs partly because the fish had disappeared but also because a great storm in November 1911 carried away most of the fishing boats and the people had been too poor to replace them.

From earliest times men were employed in the forests planted by the Campbells of Glenorchy. Even in medieval times these were coppiced for charcoal and during the eighteenh and nineteenth centuries the woodlands supplied the iron-smelting works at Ardkinglas and Bonawe. On the shores of Loch Creran, which marks the northern boundary of the parish, there are a number of charcoal-burning stances situated approximately sixty metres above the shore of the loch.

The coastal strip lent itself to cattle and sheep farming but when in the nineteenth century landowners cleared the crofts in order to make way for grazing their stock, there was little emigration from the parish. The farmworkers remained in their tenanted houses and became employed directly by the landowners in animal husbandry instead of crop growing. Mary Campbell Preston describes the twice-yearly visitation by gentlemen from Glasgow in bowler hats come to collect the rents on behalf of the absentee landlords.

In the late 1940s the Earl of Dundonald offered some of the Lochnell House lands to his sitting tenants at very reasonable prices. Other landlords followed suit so that for a time there were a number of small farms operating successfully in the area. Towards the end of the twentieth century, however, there was a move to amalgamate small farms into larger concerns so that today only one or two major landowners farm most of the peninsula.

The building in 1903 of the Ballachulish branch railway line had profound effects upon the lives of the population of Barcaldine and Benderloch. Oban became accessible to many who had never before left their home villages. As one villager was to write in later years:

Deciduous woodland suitable for coppicing (*Author's Collection*)

It is a far cry from the days when the fortnightly visit of the steamer *Lochnell* was the highlight of life on Loch Etive. No longer do the puffers from Glasgow deliver their coal cargoes to the shore twice a year, every cart and barrow in the district being commandeered to carry it away! No more are there spontaneous celebrations held on the pier at the end of a long hard day, shifting the coal. Nevertheless, the people find other ways to get together to enjoy their leisure time.

The railway was axed by Lord Beeching in 1996 when it became clear that the final section of the line to Fort William would never be completed. It was another forty years before the road could be upgraded to carry the increased load of commercial traffic resulting from the closure of the line.

Towards the end of the twentieth century a centre for the study and protection of sea life in the area was established on the loch shore between the villages of Barchaldine and Benderloch. As well as rescuing distressed animals, seals in particular, and returning them to the wild whenever possible, the organisation has created an environment in which examples of the many varieties of sea life can be displayed for the education and enjoyment of the public.

A steady decline in the rural population during the early years of the twentieth century initiated attempts to bring some additional form of permanent employment to the parish. In the 1930s, the Forestry Commision took over the foothills of the mountain range which skirts the parish to the east and planted the Benderloch and Barcaldine Forests. For a while this helped to regenerate the population but the outbreak of the Second World War again denuded the area of its young manpower. The war, however, did create a demand for seaweed products and a centuries-old industry was revived to meet the demands of twentieth-century manufacturers.

Seaweed is known to have been in use in China since 2500 BC, but the first recorded use in the western Highlands occurs in a poem said to have been written by St Columba, in which he refers to the monks of Iona collecting dulse (the red edible seaweed, *Rhodymenia palmata*) from the rocks. Dulse once provided a staple part of the crofter's diet throughout the Hebrides, either served with oatmeal in a thick broth or boiled and eaten separately with butter, its red colour adding to the otherwise rather colourless food eaten at that period and its vitamin content almost certainly acting as a satisfactory substitute for green vegetables. Carrageen (*Chondrus crispus*) was used widely in the Hebrides for making jelly-like milk puddings for invalids and infants. Crofters, noting that cattle and deer could be seen grazing on the seaweed at low tide, gathered stocks for use in winter when normal fodder was likely to be scarce. For feeding to the animals, the fuci of brown seaweeds were boiled with oatmeal, hay, chaff or oat husks as winter fodder. Black houses usually had some kind of store room attached to the house specifically for keeping the stocks of seaweed.

Varieties of fucus and laminaria have been collected from around the Hebridean Islands for centuries for use as fertiliser, the alkaline content of the plants being ideal for use on Scotland's acid soils. A crofter was often given, as a part of his tenancy, a stretch of foreshore from which he could gather seaweed for his own use.

The thickening property of seaweeds was recognised very early on and its value as a gelatinous dressing for open wounds is mentioned in several medieval medical treatsies.

In the late seventeenth century a new use was found for the species fucus. When the seaweed is burnt in a limited supply of air the product is kelp from which soda ash and potash can be extracted. These chemicals are required for the manufacture of soap and glass and are used in the process of bleaching linen, the manufacture of which was

Harvesting the coniferous forest (*Author's Collection*)

a major industry in Argyll in the eighteenth and nineteenh centuries. Kelp manufacture was a seasonal occupation in which all members of a crofting family were involved. Often whole families took their boats to outlying uninhabited islands for the season, camping out and making the kelp on the spot.

The men gathered seaweed from the shore and piled it into the narrow trenches they had prepared. Long-handled iron mallets and kelp irons were used to consolidate the mass which was then fired, using heather or wood for priming. The trench was covered with turfs to cut down oxygenation and keep out moisture. The fires were allowed to smoulder throughout the night with the womenfolk tending them until the process was complete. The following morning the kelp was broken up into reasonably sized chunks ready for transportation by sea.

At the behest of their landlords, the crofters carried out this back-breaking work during the months of June, July and August, neglecting their crofts in order to satisfy the greed of their masters. Fortunes were made by some landowners, at the expense of the health of their farm workers who suffered greatly from arthritis and strained backs as a result of their labours. It is said that on one estate on the island of Mull the sum of £15,000 was raised by kelp-making in just one season, a sum equivalent today to £750,000! Needless to say, the crofters themselves received only a minuscule portion of the riches accrued from their kelp-making. In the early 1800s the discovery of huge mineral deposits of potash near Stuttgart in Germany obviated the need for the laborious exercise of kelp-making. Entrepreneurs now sought further deposits of potash around the world and discovered them in South America and the islands of the South Pacific. The Hebridean industry which had risen so rapidly at the beginning of the century fell as quickly into decline.

In 1881 a Scottish scientist, E.C. Stanford, investigating the laminaria species of seaweed found around the coasts, isolated a group of chemicals which he called the alginates. These are jelly-like carbohydrates which have an extraordinary ability to retain water as well as possessing gelling, emulsifying and stabilising properties. In the food industry they are used to stabilise products such as meringues and ice cream, they improve the head on beer and allow the fast setting of milk-based puddings. Their emulsifying properties also make them useful in the paint, cosmetic and pharmaceutical industries. They can be spun into alkali-soluble fibres which, when incorporated into the weaving process, allow the continuous production of textile items such as stockings and handkerchiefs which can then be separated by soaking the finished product in a mild alkaline solution.

Alginate production began in Argyll when the Cefoil Company set up its plant at Campbeltown in 1932. At the outbreak of war in 1939, under the direction of the Ministry of Supply, Cefoil established further plants at Girvan, Oban and Barcaldine. During the war, owing to an absence of supplies of aluminium ore, an attempt was made to produce an alginate-based material suitable for aircraft production. A single aircraft, the Seaweed de Havilland Mosquito, was actually flown, but the material proved after all to be unstable and the project was abandoned. After the war, Cefoil became Alginate Industries Ltd. Production now concentrated upon civilian requirements and the plant at Barcaldine in particular was further developed to meet the changing needs of industry. In conjunction with the Scottish Seaweed Research Association (SSRA), there was an ongoing study into the process of obtaining and utilising seaweed products. The SSRA was wound up in the 1960s and by the 1970s only the Barcaldine plant remained on the west coast. As raw materials became more readily available elsewhere, particularly in Chile and Tasmania, the Scottish industry declined. Alginate Industries closed their doors at Barcaldine in the 1990s with the loss of many jobs. Since the present-day village of Barcaldine owes much of its development to the presence of the Cefoil factory, this was a serious blow to the burgeoning economy of the region.

Throughout the parish, attention now focuses on the tourism industry. Along the shore at Barcaldine village, boat-builders have replaced the Alginate Industries factory as major employers. Water sports and diving facilities have developed alongside a riding school. The Forestry Commission has made great strides in creating picnic areas and in opening up forest walks and bridle paths which may be used by cyclists and horse riders. Hotel and bed and breakfast accommodation is provided for tourists' needs while at the same time generating additional employment

8

LISMORE AND APPIN

*An ancient cathedral, a castle in the loch
and an unsolved murder mystery*

The Appin section of the parish of Lismore and Appin is bounded
on the south and east by Loch Creran and Loch Baile together
with the upper reaches of Glen Creran. To the north, the boundary
is formed by Loch Leven and to the west by Loch Linnhe. The
northernmost tip of the island of Lismore is approximately one
mile from Port Appin and is approached across a narrow strait by
a pedestrian ferry. The island, which is some nine miles in length,
is also serviced by a vehicular ferry from Oban whose terminal on
Lismore is at Achnachroish midway along the eastern shore.

The entire parish is thus surrounded by natural barriers which
must have given some consolation to the inhabitants during times
of unrest. The villages here are widely dispersed and few in number,
Port Appin, Appin, Portnacroish, Keil and Duror being the principal
developments on the mainland while the island of Lismore may be
regarded as a single entity. Until the coming of the railway in 1903,
there was no crossing of Loch Creran other than by ferry while the
mouth of Loch Leven was not bridged until the 1970s. The alternative
was to make a long diversion around the head of either loch. The
insular nature of the territory may also account for the independence
of thought and action taken by the people over the centuries, many
clinging to the Church of Rome despite the penalties imposed by
successive rulers. These differences of opinion often resulted in
conflict with authority and created a colourful chronicle of events
in the parish.

The area was greatly affected by the Ice Age when sea levels fell
drastically, as witnessed by the raised beaches at Port Appin,
Portnacroish and Cuil Bay. The severity of the winters in Neolithic
times must have driven any human population far to the south for
there is little evidence of early man until the return of the Picts,
when the climate began to warm up. Evidence abounds of Celtic

occupation, however, from the first to the sixth century AD including sites of a number of brochs in the area. The broch known as Tirefour Castle on Lismore, dating from *c.* 100 BC, is a prominent feature in the landscape. Standing on a limestone ridge above Port Moluag, it is one of the best-preserved prehistoric monuments of its kind in Argyll.

The broch was an invention of the Celts. It consists of a circular tower with double-skinned outer wall and contained within the walls a stairway to the next level. The ground-floor space is believed to have been occupied by cattle in times of siege although some doubts have been cast upon this theory in recent times. The higher levels were floored in timbers providing shelter for the chieftain, his family and retainers. The broch at Tirefour encloses an inner space of 12.2 m diameter. The remaining walls stand to about 3 m.

The Christian era began with the arrival of St Moluag on Lismore in 563. The island was no doubt chosen at that time because of its fertile soil which is derived from the limestone of which the island is largely composed. Legend has it that both St Columba and St Moluag arriving in Loch Linnhe, *c.* 563, fancied Lismore as a centre for their missionary work amongst the Picts. The priests approached the island in separate boats, racing to be the first to land and establish the right to the territory. Saint Moluag, cutting off one finger, tossed it onto the beach ahead of Columba's boat, crying 'My flesh and blood have first possession of the island and I bless it in the name of the Lord!'

It is thought that it was St Moluag who established the religious community on the island although there is little recorded information about his life. What is believed to have been his pastoral staff, the bachuil mor, is held in trust by the occupants of Bachuil House. The original chapel of St Moluag was to become an abbey and church and the settlement servicing the abbey would have been the first village in the area. The abbey church was raised to the status of a cathedral between 1183 and 1189 when the Church of Rome superseded the Celtic Church and a new diocese of Argyll was formed.

With a small population and few external resources, the cathedral never flourished and was several times bailed out by grants from Rome. Within fifty or sixty years there were strenuous efforts to establish a cathedral on mainland Argyll which would be more accessible to the entire diocese. As a consequence of the indecision about its future, the cathedral was poorly maintained. It seldom fulfilled its diocesan role, and despite having survived the Reformation, it was allowed to fall into disrepair.

Despite St Moluag's position as the parish church of Appin and Lismore it was generally only the islanders who attended services there. From the fifteenth century onwards the villages on the mainland were served by a chapel built at Keil in the north of the parish and, from 1641, by a second church at Tynribbie lying on the Oban–Fort William road at its junction with the road to Appin. Once the people of Appin and Duror had been provided with their own churches they no longer expected to maintain St Moluag's and it was left to the island population to support its church alone. This they failed to do and eventually a smaller church building was constructed within the cathedral walls which served as a church for the island population. The original plan of the cathedral, a narrow oblong *c.* 40 m long and *c.* 7.5 m in width, consisted of nave and choir. After the Reformation the choir served as the parish church while the nave was allowed to collapse into ruin. In 1749 a major reconstruction of the parish church introduced round-arched windows on the south-facing wall and galleries were inserted. The pulpit was moved to the south wall and worship thereby reorientated. In 1900 further changes returned the pulpit to the west wall and round-arched windows were inserted in the north wall. Only the east gallery was retained but a new roof with impressive bell tower was added. There are remnants of the medieval church in the piscina, triple-arched sedilia and the pulpit arch in the west gable. The graveyard contains a number of burial slabs of the fourteenth and fifteenth centuries together with a carved tomb-chest lid of sixteenth-century origin. White marble funerary tablets of the eighteenth century have been built into the east wall of the church.

Thomas Pennant visited Lismore in 1772 and reported a population of 1,500 inhabitants. He spoke of the island having once been a great garden but also at some time in the past a deer forest. He remarks upon the extraordinary number of stag horns dug up in the area of the old deer forest. It is known that the young King James IV was a frequent visitor to Stalker Castle where he came for the hunting. Perhaps it was on Lismore that the chase took place?

Pennant was unimpressed by the agricultural expertise of the islanders at the end of the eighteenth century. He reports the agricultural land as having been overused, with little attempt made to fertilise it despite the ready supplies of seaweed and lime available. He points out, however, that it is no longer possible for the people to burn the limestone as all the forests have been destroyed.

The main crops of the island were at this time bere and oats. The

Illicit whisky still, eighteenth century (*copyright © RCAHMS*)

oats were generally used in the payment of rents and since whisky distilling took all the bere produced, it was necessary for the people to import meal for household use. Thomas Pennant roundly condemns the profligacy of those who would starve, rather than forgo the opportunity of making whisky!

One hundred head of cattle were exported annually from Lismore in 1772 and many horses were bred. According to Pennant, the horses did not do well. They were put to work at the age of two to three years, but quickly lost their teeth and subsequently died from starvation. Was this perhaps something to do with the quality of the water on the island? There were three small lochans, two supporting large populations of trout and one, exclusively, eels.

Pennant considered the people of Lismore to be 'very poor. They are troubled with sore eyes and in springtime they are afflicted with a costiveness [constipation] that often proves fatal.' Again one wonders if the water was to blame. Today's island population is served by water piped across, undersea, from the mainland.

In 1803 the Roman Catholic Church founded a Highland College on Lismore with the intention of educating boys for the priesthood. In order to finance the enterprise, Bishop John Chisholm opened lime quarries on the island and had kilns built for burning the lime. He also engaged the local farmers to produce food for the school.

Sir Walter Scott, having sailed past the island in 1814, commented: 'Reports speak well of the lime but indifferently of the students.' The limeworks did not yield the income that Chisholm had anticipated and, unable to afford good teachers or to attract the sons of the rich nobility, his pupils did not achieve acceptable standards and were eventually transferred to a seminary in the Lowlands.

Despite its importance to the early Christian missionaries as fertile farmland and its value as a source of limestone, today the island of Lismore can boast no settlement larger than the township of Port Ramsay.

By 1800 the population of Lismore was 1,740, many of whom found employment in the lime-burning industry. There are groups of workers' cottages and disused limekilns at Port Kilcheran, An Sailean and Port Ramsay are all that remains of an important industry.

The clearances of the nineteenth century were accompanied by a steady decline in the lime-burning industry, and this resulted in a rapid reduction in population to fewer than one hundred in the 1930s. The introduction of salmon farming during the 1980s, together with improvements in ferry access, in particular a regular vehicular service from Oban, have made living on the island a viable proposition. Today the population is 175 and rising.

The importance of shipping in this area can never be exaggerated. From earliest times the sea had been the only manner of travelling from one major settlement in Argyll to another. Discoveries of Viking boats and ship-burials in and around Oban in the late nineteenth century confirm the presence in these waters of the Norsemen during the eleventh and twelfth centuries. Those summoned to the seat of power in Inverary must either have travelled by sea or faced a dangerous and lengthy journey on foot or horseback. By the turn of the eighteenth century, the seaways of the Inner Hebrides were cluttered with shipping and so treacherous were the seas in stormy weather that many vessels were lost. In 1833 Alan Stevenson was commissioned to build a lighthouse on the islet of Musdile at the southernmost tip of Lismore. A single-arched stone bridge now connects Musdile with Lismore island but for long the keepers were obliged to negotiate the narrow but difficult crossing by boat. For nearly 200 years there were two keepers and their families living here in this most inaccessible part of the parish. Today the light is operated automatically and the keepers' cottages have been converted into a private dwelling house.

Alan Stevenson's lighthouse on Musdile Isle, Lismore (*Author's Collection*)

The name Appin derives from the Gaelic Apuin (Abbey lands). The Strath of Appin is a broad band of low-lying, fertile country protected from the worst of the wintry gales by the mountains of Morvern to the west and those of Glen Coe to the east. No doubt when Lismore Abbey held sway in the area, this land would have been worked for the benefit of the Abbey itself and its occupants. As the population increased and more and more of the fertile land came under the plough, villages grew up further to the north of the parish at Duror and Kentallen.

The parish survived the Viking era virtually unscathed and it was not until King Hakon fled the scene after the Battle of Largs in 1263 that local clans began to fight amongst themselves for territorial advantage. It was at this time that they saw the serious necessity of erecting strongholds such as Castle Stalker in Loch Laich, Achadun Castle on Lismore and Glensanda Castle in Morvern.

Achadun, dating from the twelfth century, was the first of these to be built. Of the original castle nothing now remains but a curtain wall enclosing a square courtyard. Castle Stalker is believed to have been erected upon the site of an earlier stronghold and was built about 1320 by the MacDougall Lords of Lorn. Castle Stalker, much restored and refurbished from its fourteenth-century beginnings, is still inhabited to this day.

In 1388 the Lordship of Lorn passed to the Clan Stewart. They occupied the MacDougalls' original stronghold in Loch Laich until 1446 when it was rebuilt by Sir John Stewart, Lord of Lorn.

Castle Stalker is an oblong tower which occupies most of a small island in Loch Laich accessible by a causeway at low tide. The main approach to the tower is by a formidable forestair built against the north-east wall. This was begun in the late seventeenth century but only completed in 1909. There is another entrance at ground level leading into vaulted cellars. The tower rises three storeys to a gabled garret with parapet walks and round towers in the angles, all of which are capped with slated cones. Although it has undergone extensive repairs on a number of occasions down the centuries, Castle Stalker remains much as it was after alterations in the fifteenth century. The building is supposed to be one of the earliest in Scotland to have been roofed using Easdale slates.

In 1540 Sir John Stewart became the father of an illegitimate son. Determined to make him his legal heir, Sir John arranged to marry the child's mother, a member of the Clan MacLaren. As he made his way to the chapel at Dunstaffnage on his wedding day, Sir John was attacked and mortally wounded by Alan MacCoul, a renegade MacDougall. MacCoul's intention to kill Sir John before he could legitimise his heir was thwarted, however, for despite his wounds Sir John insisted upon continuing with the marriage, thus preventing the McDougalls from regaining the title, Lord of Lorn. Sir John's son, Dugald, became the first Stewart Chief of Appin.

Sir John had anticipated trouble with the MacDougalls over the inheritance of the Lordship of Lorn, so he established a stronghold capable of protecting his wife and family. Chosing Castle Stalker for this purpose, he set about improving its defences. The young laird, Dugald Stewart, grew up determined to avenge his father's murder. In 1468, with an army comprised of Stewarts and MacLarens, he fought a battle against the MacDougalls at Stalc, on the mainland opposite Castle Stalker. Alan MacCoul was slain during the battle, probably by Dugald himself. The site is marked by a stone which stands today beside the churchyard at Portnacroish.

Dugald Stewart died in 1497 in a raid carried out against the MacDonalds of Keppoch, as a reprisal for cattle stealing. He was succeeded by his son, Duncan. With the murders of Duncan Stewart by the MacLeans at Duart Castle in 1512 and of Sir Alexander Stewart by Campbells in 1520, the Stewart clan found itself engaged in a continuous and bloody feud with its neighbours.

The new laird was a cousin and boyhood companion to the young King James IV of Scotland. The King came frequently to Appin for the hunting and it is thought that additions were made to the castle at this time to accommodate the royal visitor. The royal coat of arms is displayed above the front door and the name Castle Stalker appears to have arisen from its use at this time as the King's hunting lodge.

During the 1745 Rising James Stewart, Laird of Ardsheal, joined the Jacobite cause and Castle Stalker, together with all the Stewart lands, was confiscated by the crown. The castle was put into the charge of the Duke of Argyll who assigned his own kinsman to its stewardship. The Stewarts retreated to their family seat at Ardsheal, near Duror.

Throughout 1745 and 1746, Castle Stalker was a garrison for troops stationed there to discourage any Jacobite movement along the west coast. James Stewart nevertheless joined his kinsman, Prince Charles Edward Stewart, on his victorious march into England and fought beside him at the battle of Culloden. After the defeat of the Jacobite forces, Stewart fled to France leaving his wife and seven children to the mercy of Major-General John Campbell of Mamor, later to become the 4th Duke of Argyll.

Before marching north to receive the surrender of the Highland Chieftains, the Major-General did what he could to relieve the suffering of dependents of those killed or imprisoned after the battle. The man he appointed to act as steward to the Appin estates during his absence was one Captain Scott, a fanatical Presbyterian determined to carry out, without mercy, his orders to search out renegades amongst the Appin people. Disregarding his General's order to treat the people sympathetically, he ravaged the villages, destroying crops, confiscating cattle and valuables and burning the houses. When he marched into the estate of the exiled Clan Chief, Stewart of Ardsheal, he removed all the provisions and cattle which had previously been allocated by the Major General to help the laird's family through the winter. Scott also attempted to remove Lady Ardsheal and her children from the house but here he met his match. Lady Ardsheal refused to budge and instead sent a message to Major-General Campbell imploring his assistance. As a consequence, Scott was ordered to leave the family unmolested. Nevertheless before he departed, he stripped the house of everything worth taking including the fine oak panelling, roofing slates and lintels. He intended to destroy the house by fire but the stone construction withstood the onslaught and the laird's house was later restored in time to receive the master on his return from exile. James Stewart remained at Ardsheal and the village of Duror grew up in support of the mansion.

With the removal of the infamous Captain Scott, the man now charged with overseeing the Appin estates was one Colin Campbell of Glenure, a kinsman of the Duke of Argyll. Colin Campbell was not, at first, a malevolent character. He carried out his duties humanely, being as lenient as possible with those who were unable to pay their rents. After some years of very poor returns, however, the authorities began to lean on him to extract more revenue from the parish and in order to save his own skin he was forced to become more demanding in his dealings with the people. His uncharacteristic harshness aroused a great deal of resentment within the parish, culminating in his assassination on 14 May 1752, the attack taking place near Ballachulish, in the woods at Lettermore.

The murder of a government officer so incensed the authorities that they determined to prosecute someone for the crime, guilty or not. Suspicion fell upon James Stewart of Acharn, James of the Glen.

James Stewart was tried by the Duke of Argyll at Inverary before a jury consisting of eleven Campbells and four others. Although this might appear to have been a rigged jury, one must appreciate that it would probably have been impossible, at that time, to find sufficient people in Argyll, eligible for jury service, whose name was not Campbell! With no evidence other than hearsay and a vague eyewitness description of the perpetrator, James was found guilty and sentenced to death. He was hanged on a gibbet set up at the scene of the crime, overlooking Loch Leven. As a dire warning to others, his body was left to rot for three years before members of the Stewart clan were allowed to remove it and inter the remains in the Chapel of Keil in Duror.

From then on, Campbells resided in Castle Stalker until 1800 at which time it was in a ruinous state and was abandoned in favour of a new house which had been built at Airds Bay on the mainland. In 1840, the roof either collapsed or was removed to avoid paying taxes. Thereafter, the building was little more than a ruin when, in 1908, Charles Stewart of Achara purchased it and carried out some restoration work. In 1965, Lt.-Colonel D.R. Stewart Allward, purchased the property and with his own hands and with the help of family and friends began a ten-year project to restore the castle to a habitable building and a family home.

The village of Appin, which is the only substantial settlement in the whole parish, is divided into Port Appin which occupies a narrow stretch of shoreline opposite Lismore Island, and Appin village itself which lies perhaps a kilometre to the north. At Port Appin overlooking the jetty for the Lismore passenger ferry stands the early nineteenth-century ferry house which consists of two bow-fronted cottages with a boat-house between. Nearby stands the nineteenth-century Airds Hotel, originally an inn serving travellers to and from Lismore.

Outside the village, Airds House was built in 1738–9 in the Palladian style with a pedimented three-storey centre portion topped with urns and with wings to either side. The walls are harled, their margins elaborately dressed. The home farm and lodge are of early nineteenth-century origin. In 1746, Airds House was chosen as the site of a large government camp, set up as a base for General Campbell's troops as they swept northwards, accepting, one by one, the surrender of the Highland chieftains.

In Appin village there is a row of cottages dating from the late eighteenth and early nineteenth century which include the post office, a plain rectangular building with chimneyed gables, and a pair of cottages once thatched but now roofed in corrugated iron. Other houses are of later date, many from the twentieth century. The ruins of the old parish church, built most probably on the foundations of an older church, are dated 1749 and indicate an original oblong structure later extended into a T-plan during the nineteenth century. Still surviving are a segmental arched door and a forestair.

At Portnacroish a little to the north and straddling the main road to Fort William, buildings are of the late eighteenth and early nineteenth century. They include a post office, a forge, an old inn and a byre.

In 1803 William and Dorothy Wordsworth stopped here on their journey through the Highlands and William speaks of 'an indifferent inn by the side of the loch'. Dorothy, however, waxes lyrical about the scenery: 'A covering of cloud rested on the long range of hills of Morvern. Mists floated very near the water . . . yet the sky was clear and the sea from the reflection of sky, was of an ethereal, sapphire blue. Green islands lay on the calm water . . . islands far greener, for so it seemed, than the grass of other places . . .'

The Episcopalian Church of the Holy Cross was built in 1815. This simple structure with its three pointed-arch windows in the south front has undergone numerous interior reconstructions but is now in very much the same condition as when it was built originally. The village stands overlooking Castle Stalker and its origins appear to be associated with the construction of Appin House early in the eighteenth century.

Castle Stalker being considered no longer suitable as a family house, the Stewart laird decided to build a mansion in the style of the period, classic in line and possibly pedimented. Little remains of the original Appin House, however, which was erected upon the foundations of a much earlier Stewart stronghold. The house was much altered in 1831 when a new front with a balustraded parapet was added and in 1960 all was demolished save the south-east wing which

Stewart graves in Keil Churchyard, Duror (*Author's Collection*)

now constitutes the principal apartment of a modern dwelling house designed by the David Newman Partnership.

The village of Duror in the north of the parish grew up around an early Christian cell probably built on the site later occupied by the medieval chapel of Keil, a kilometre from the present village of Duror itself. Dedicated to St Columba and built in 1354, this chapel is thought to have been still in use in 1630 although no specific records exist from this period. Now only a remnant of the chapel wall remains in the churchyard which contains some stones of great antiquity. The oldest decipherable tombstone, however, is dated 1707. The stone of Duncan MacColl, who died at the age of seventy-five in 1822, has carvings of a shotgun and hound, suggesting that perhaps he was a gamekeeper or a sportsman. The 1825 stone of John MacDougall of Ballachulish and his wife Rachel MacColl, shows that she had three children and bore five still-born babies. The inscription is Vigilante Hora Vent (be watchful for the hour cometh). The northern section of the churchyard contains a large collection of Stewart graves, dating from the eighteenth century onwards.

Duror Parish Church which stands on the southern edge of the village was built in 1827. This a parliamentary kirk built to a design of the architect James Smith of Inverness and approved by Thomas Telford. Such churches were erected by order of the government in Westminster in order to appease the unrest amongst church-goers at this time culminating, nevertheless, in the Disruption of 1843.

Perhaps the most noticeable feature of this tiny village is its twentieth-century community hall which seems strangely disproportionate, its rather grand portico inconsistent with the traditional cottages alongside it.

The parish of Appin and Lismore was to remain isolated from the remainder of Argyll until the beginning of the nineteenth century when, following the opening of the Crinan Canal and the introduction of paddle steamers on the west coast, travel between Glasgow and Fort William came within reach of the lowliest of parishioners. A pier was built at Port Appin to accommodate the steamers which called daily, sailing once in either direction.

Travel into and out of the parish was further encouraged by the opening, in 1903, of the Callander & Oban Railway branch line to Ballachulish. The route had originally been planned to link Oban with Inverness via Fort William but once Loch Etive and Loch Creran had been bridged and the track had reached the southern shore of Loch Leven, further construction came to an abrupt end. Faced with continuous wrangling about the bridge planned to cross the . narrows between South and North Ballachulish, the Callander & Oban Railway Company lost patience with the procrastination of Argyll Council and the self-interest expressed by both the Slate Quarrying Company and the Inverleven Aluminium Works. The Railway Company withdrew from the contract, extending the line only as far as the pier of the easternmost slate quarry at East Laroch.

It was to be another sixty years before road traffic could cross Loch Leven at its mouth without waiting in a queue for the tediously slow and woefully inadequate vehicular ferry. The new steel road bridge was completed in 1975 to a pattern reminiscent of the Connel Bridge and one which blends comfortably with the surrounding landscape.

The opening of the railway had a significant impact upon the community at the start of the twentieth century. Those seeking employment in Oban could now commute from Appin and even Lismore. Visitors to the area found the railway a pleasant alternative to sea travel, particularly in winter and tourism began to boost the economy of the parish. To accommodate visitors making their way northwards a magnificent new hotel was built beside Appin railway station. This was followed shortly by others, cashing in on the influx of visitors.

The social life of the village changed dramatically when an additional train was introduced late at night on a Saturday. This meant that people could find their entertainment in the flesh-pots of Oban and still get home in time for church on Sunday! Those obliged to change trains for the branch line at Connel might wait in the bar of the Falls of Lora Hotel. When the driver was ready to set out upon his final run of the day across the Connel Bridge, he hooted loudly to warn the passengers and, before setting off, would wait until the very last inebriate had boarded the train, with or without the assistance of his friends.

There had been public schools in both Appin and at Duror since the early nineteenth century but there was no provision for secondary education. With the coming of the railway, children in the parish were able to travel into Oban daily. There are reminiscences of these train journeys from Duror and Appin in *Oban High School – The First 100 Years*, produced for the school's centenary.

Creagan Inn (*Author's Collection*)

When, in the 1890s, the people heard that the railway would span all three lochs at their narrowest point, there was great rejoicing at the prospect of shorter journeys on foot, back and forth. The Railway Company went into negotiations with Argyll Council to provide on each of the bridges, a roadway or at least a footpath for local use, running alongside the railway track. The Council, however, refused to pay the 2 or 300 pounds demanded by the Company for the construction and upkeep of these walkways and the cost of link roads to either end of the bridges. Creagan bridge was built without vehicular access and the footpaths which were provided were restricted to use by railway workers only. Officially, those pedestrians wishing to cross the bridge were obliged to purchase a ticket for a two-mile journey and to board and leave the train at a conveniently sited station. From the well-beaten paths leading up onto the bridge however, it was clear that many an illegal crossing took place after dark, in particular one supposes to and from the old coaching inn to the north of the Creagan Bridge!

The Callander & Oban Railway had bridged Loch Etive and Loch Creran at the mouth, reducing the road distance to Appin by many miles. Road traffic, however, was still obliged to use a ferry or to take

New Creagan Bridge (*Author's Collection*)

the circuitous route around the head of each of the lochs. Had the railway reached Fort William and linked Oban with Inverness, it is unlikely that Lord Beeching would have declared the line redundant in 1966. As it was, a facility which had proved a lifeline to the parish gave way to road transport.

At Connel the steel rails were removed and the bridge converted to carry vehicular traffic. Conversion of the Creagan Bridge, however, was considered too costly. The bridge was allowed to fall into such a state of decay that when, in the 1990s, it was at last decided to take the road across the loch at its mouth, the old bridge had to be demolished before a new structure was put in its place!

Traditionally the occupation of this region was farming and fishing, the large estates being divided up into family-managed crofts, but during the eighteenth century the landscape was to suffer irreversible change as a result of the industrial revolution. The introduction of ironworks at Bonawe resulted in an enormous demand for charcoal from throughout the region and in north Appin, the ancient oak forests were denuded to be replaced, a hundred years later, by an unsightly regimental planting of pine and fir by the Forestry Commission.

When, during the Napoleonic Wars, wool, mutton and beef were in demand to clothe and feed the armed forces, such high prices were offered to landowners that the small farms and crofts around Duror and Kentallen were swept away to make way for sheep and cattle. The pattern of the landscape changed from small, neatly dyked or fenced-in fields into open grasslands where cattle grazed in the lower-lying pastures and sheep were scattered across the open foothills. Those parishioners removed from the land went elsewhere and the population dwindled. Only the opening of the slate quarries at Ballachulish and, in the twentieth century, the introduction of aluminium processing at Kinlochleven were to provide any substantial form of employment. With the expansion of tourism following the Second World War, the population has increased to cater for visitors' needs. Small businesses of every kind have sprung up in the parish, each one giving employment to just a few people. In total, however, this represents a substantial workforce. The resulting boost to the economy of the district can be seen in the substantial amount of refurbishment of old property which has taken place in recent years and the building of new, albeit small, housing developments.

9

MORVERN AND ARDNAMURCHAN

Lead shot for Wellington and winkles for London's East End

Until the regionalisation of Scotland in 1976 Ardnamurchan, Morvern and Ardgour were part of the County of Argyll. Because of their close association with the county in the past, these parishes are included in this account.

Morvern and Ardnamurchan consist of some of the wildest and most remote territory of the British Isles. Until the 1960s there was no through road suitable for carrying the heavy traffic which had landed from the Corran ferry, any further north than the village of Acharacle at the head of Loch Shiel.

The land is heavily indented all along its coastline creating a succession of peninsulas, the sea effectively cutting each landmass off from the others. Along each there is a single road and although well surfaced and properly maintained, these are largely single track with passing places. Even today the more remote villages are more easily accessed by ferry from Mull than by road.

There is evidence of human settlement in Morvern and Ardnamurchan as early as 4000 BC but the most convincing remains, in west Ardnamurchan near Achosnich (the field of the sighing winds), are of Bronze Age (2000 BC onwards). In a valley between Achosnich and Sonachan, at the spot known as Cnoc Nitheadrechd, are signs of a very early settlement and in Achosnich itself a stone axe dating from 2000 BC was discovered in 1952. At Sonachan a millstone of approximately the same age was also found. To the earliest settlers the rocky promontories and sheltered sandy bays around these shores offered safe harbours and strongholds which could be defended against both wild animals and human aggressors. Cairns, barrows and hill forts all tell their story of human endeavour to eke out an existence in this wild, remote landscape.

In earlier times, streams and lochs teemed with game fish while the oak woods provided timber for heating and shelter and harboured all manner of game. There is evidence of wild boar, wolves and bear having roamed these woodlands and even today red deer, wild cat

Red deer stag (*Author's Collection*)

and pine marten, extinct in most parts of the British Isles, breed here and live unmolested in the wildlife sanctuaries designated by Scottish Natural Heritage. Within the ancient deciduous woodlands and the dark pine forests planted during the twentieth century, along the shore and above the tree line, one may see some of the rarest of Britain's birds. The deep sea lochs with their many sheltered inlets once provided a rich harvest of fish while the shoreline yielded up its bounty of shellfish and edible seaweed. The volcanic rocks of the region, weathered and redistributed by water and ice have formed pockets of fertile ground in sheltered valleys and along the raised beaches of the last Ice Age. Here there grew up several small crofting communities which still exist, townships which were the nucleus of today's villages.

For many centuries the peninsulas of Ardnamurchan and Morvern were subjected to invasion, first from Ireland and later by the Vikings.

In the sixth century AD there was an influx of Scoti from Ireland and Ardnamurchan was peopled by Dalriads, Scoti who had already colonised the southern parts of Dalriada (Argyll). Saint Columba is said to have made several visits to Ardnamurchan after he had established himself on Iona. Adamnan who was St Columba's chronicler recorded that (at this time) 'the Irish immigrants had the freedom of Ardnamurchan'. There are several references to Columba in place-names such as Torbar Chalum Chille (St Columba's well) and Eilean Chalium Chille (St Columba's isle).

The ecclesiastical centre of Ardnamurchan has from earliest times been Kilchoan, the name being derived from Cill Chomhghain (Comgan's cell). Chomhghain was the son of a prince of Leinster who came from Ireland with Kentigern and Fillan towards the end of the seventh century.

Towards the end of the eighth century Vikings arrived from Denmark (Fionnghaill – the fair strangers) and from Norway (Dubhghaill – the dark strangers) colonised and intermarried. By 1079 Godred Crobhan ruled the Norse Kingdom of the Isles which stretched from Shetland to the Isle of Man. While Ardnamurchan was relatively peaceful during this period there is evidence from place-names that Norsemen resided here. Suffixes such as -dale, -vat, -vik, and -ness all arising from this source. From a mixed marriage of Viking with Scots arose the great leader of the twelfth century, Somerled, who spent his early life in Morvern. Appointed leader of the men of Morvern, he defeated Norwegian settlers living on the peninsula, killing among others one Borrodill who was said to have been a giant of a man, some seven feet tall. Glenborrodale undoubtedly takes its name from him. Somerled had many famous victories before taking the title King of the Isles. In order to bring stability to the situation he married Ragnhildis, the daughter of King Olaf the Red, of the Isle of Man and the Sudereys. A peace treaty signed in 1156 gave Somerled all of the land south of Ardnamurchan leaving everything to the north in the hands of the Vikings. In 1266, Somerled's grandson, Angus Mor, repossessed Ardnamurchan and when he was granted a Royal Charter in 1284 he passed it to his son, John Sprangaich. John gave rise to the Clan MacIain (son of John). The MacIains controlled the peninsula by reconstructing a fortification on an existing earthworks at Mingary Castle, near Kilchoan. Constructed of local stone, the ruins show evidence of a substantial drawbridge which, when raised, would have made the castle impregnable. Unfortunately much of the structure has been destroyed, the stone perhaps being used for buildings in the settlements close by. It is believed that Castle Tioram in Moidart, the seat of the MacDonald Lords of the Isles, is of the same age.

King David II renewed the Charter in 1344 and the MacIains continued to support their overlords, the MacDonald Lords of the Isles, contributing to many victories including the battle of Inverlochy in which the Earl of Argyll's forces were defeated. King James IV visited Mingary in 1493 and 1495 when he received oaths of loyalty from the major clan chiefs. MacIain's loyalty was rewarded when he received a direct Crown Charter for the lands of Ardnamurchan but on the death of James IV at Flodden in 1513, state power was weakened in the west of Scotland and feuding between the clans began once again. Following a series of battles with the Macdonalds who had designs on the peninsula, many of the male leaders of the MacIains were killed leaving a female heir, Mariot. The clan at first agreed to appoint Mariot's cousin Alasdair, as her adviser and the leader of her army but he had already aligned himself with Sir Donald Macdonald of Lochalsh, a known rebel whose lands were forfeit to the Crown. Fearing the same for Ardnamurchan, the clan chose the lesser evil, resigning the Ardnamurchan lands in favour of Archibald Campbell, 4th Earl of Argyll. The Campbells controlled the region until the nineteenth century when the Duke of Argyll withdrew from this part of his vast domain and the lands were sold off as individual estates to wealthy industrialists from the south.

The first minister for Ardnamurchan, Donald Omey, was appointed in 1624. His parish church was at Kilchoan although his residence was probably on Eilean Fhaonaan in Loch Shiel. According to Craven in his *Records of Argyll and the Isles*, Omey was appointed by the Bishop of Argyll, Andrew Boyd, in the hope that this learned and godly priest would put a stop to the warring between the clans. Unfortunately the Chief of Clanranald would have none of it. He sent his henchman to address the priest while he was conducting as service in the church. He told him to 'leave forthwith or die!' Omey left the parish in 1629 although whether this was as a result of Clanranald's intimidation is not known. Later that same year Duncan McCalman, a Protestant minister, was appointed by Sir Donald Campbell. Despite the hostility of the locals who resented the removal of Omey, McCalman eventually won over his parishioners and served them as their minister until in 1650 he was excommunicated for associating with other rebellious priests. He died in 1672. A number of colourful characters were to hold the post over the centuries several of whom

Ardnamurchan Parish Church, Kilchoan (*Author's Collection*)

were in trouble for their political alliances. One, Daniel MacLauchlan, was charged in 1733 with intemperance and profanity when he was overheard singing indecent songs; the following year these charges were dismissed. However, Daniel was clearly a much misunderstood gentleman for he soon found himself imprisoned in King's Bench Prison in London, in July 1735, accused of being the author of 'A vile, abominable and obscene pamphlet dedicated to a noble peer'. His pamphlet, a serious attempt to explore and rectify the problems of inbreeding amongst the aristocratic families in the realm, was entitled 'Improving and Adding to the Strength of Great Britain and Northern Island by Fornication'.

During the ministry of Kenneth MacCauley, appointed in 1761, a new parish church was built. Now a roofless shell, it stands on elevated ground some 400 m from the present church. The eighteenth-century construction incorporates parts of an earlier medieval building and it is very possible that a place of Christian worship has stood on this same site since the sixth century. The cemetery contains a long flat stone carved with Celtic designs which local tradition suggests came originally from Iona.

By 1827, during the ministry of Angus Maclean, the old church was in a poor condition and the decision was taken to build a new church and manse on a fresh site, the land being given by Sir James Riddel who also contributed 200 pounds to the cost of building. The church is built to a T-plan with side galleries and a Laird's loft facing the pulpit, so that the preacher and the laird are at the same level above the congregation. The Laird's loft was carpeted and furnished with arm chairs and a couch. Until quite recently, the separate townships in the parish each had their own specified pews. After the Disruption of 1843, a Free Church was also built in the village.

By the twentieth century, the lairds of true Highland origin had mostly disappeared and been replaced by gentlemen seeking a country retreat where they might entertain their sporting friends. It was the advent of these new landowners which brought about the most catastrophic changes for the crofting communities of Ardnamurchan. The most profitable kind of farming requiring the least outlay and a minimum of labour is sheep rearing. To make way for the flocks, many of the smaller crofting villages were cleared and the people moved further along the peninsula to begin again in Kilchoan and its associated settlements of Portuairk, Achnaha, Ockle and Kilmory.

Although there had been settlement this far west since pre-Reformation times, it had never been considered a place where farming would be successful. While Kilchoan itself offered a well-protected bay with fine sandy beaches and a wide stretch of low-lying, fertile ground, the other settlements were on the more exposed north-western part of the peninsula where the soil was poor and the weather conditions relentless.

There is a distinct contrast here with the deep-sided leafy valleys further to the east. Open moorland covers the hills which have been denuded of trees by the gales sweeping in from the Atlantic. Small groups of houses crouch in the valleys along the shoreline gaining what protection they can find from the jagged headlands of volcanic rock. There is little to encourage the serious farmer. Crofters who had made a reasonable living further inland found themselves struggling to survive. Towards the middle of the nineteenth century there was a general exodus, many families facing the challenge of life on the other side of the globe rather than battle against impossible odds. The two world wars offered those young people who remained a chance to escape their rigorous existence. Many of those who survived the conflict never returned to the crofts.

At the time of the clearances, Kilchoan provided a living for twenty-two crofters. Families removed from Bourblaig on the eastern flank of Ben Hiant were resettled at Plocaig by Sanna. A very honest and at times harrowing account of the problems faced by the crofters at Sanna is given in Alasdair Maclean's book, *Night Falls on Ardnamurchan*.

On a rocky promontory, the farthest west point of the British Isles, stands Ardnamurchan Lighthouse. Established in 1849, it was built by Alan Stevenson, the uncle of Robert Louis Stevenson. With a candlepower of 550,000 candles, its nominal range is twenty-four miles. Today it is controlled automatically and regularly maintained by engineers working for the Commissioners of Northern Lighthouses, but in earlier times a small community grew up here around the light. Substantial stone houses provided accommodation for the keepers and their families and below the lighthouse, in sheltered gullies, can be seen the stone-walled gardens which sustained them.

The nearby township of Plocaig is now deserted, only crumbling stone walls and the outlines of a few of the runrigs remain. Sanna cove, having the benefit of a beautiful beach of white sand and some spectacular sand-dunes, is a great attraction for holidaymakers. A small group of holiday cottages together with the houses of a few permanent inhabitants are all that remain of the original crofting township.

The fate of those tenants who had been ousted from family crofts going back many generations was eventually aired in Parliament and in 1886 an outraged House of Commons passed the Crofts Holdings (Scotland) Act, which guaranteed security of tenure for families. It was too late for the people of west Ardnamurchan, however, where many of the men went away to sea in order to support those left behind on the crofts. At one time it was said that the tiny village of Portuairk could boast eight sea captains from among its inhabitants. Duncan Cameron, the river pilot who, in 1938, navigated the Cunard liner *Queen Mary* from John Brown's shipyard down the Clyde to the open sea, was born at Kilchoan. After the Second World War he was brought out of retirement to do the same for the *Queen Elizabeth*.

In the early days following the clearances when many crofters were resettled in the area, each small township had its own school and place of worship. In some cases this was a small hall, little better

Ardnamurchan Lighthouse (*Author's Collection*)

than a byre. As the population became depleted the schools were amalgamated at Kilchoan. In 1961 there were thirty pupils attending in the care of two teachers while at Kilmory, the only other village to retain its own school, there were only eight children with one teacher. By 2000 all the children of west Ardnamurchan attended school in Kilchoan.

The principal landowner on the peninsula of Ardnamurchan at the beginning of the twentieth century was C.D. Rudd who, in 1900, built Glenborrodale Castle on land associated with the much older township of Glenborrodale. In compliance with the Education Act in 1872 a school was built here to accommodate the children within three to five miles' walking distance. The building also served the function of a church and is thought to be the only school in Argyll with a pulpit in the classroom! Today it is still in use as a school for younger children and remains in use as the centre for all village activities.

Until late in the twentieth century, the main access to the villages of west Ardnamurchan was by sea. Even holidaymakers found it easier to bring their cars by ferry via Mull to Kilchoan. In the early days, all supplies came in by MacBrayne's steamers, the vessels anchoring in the bay while the local ferrymen rowed cargo and passengers ashore. In a rough sea it could be a perilous approach for visitors.

In 1890 there was a proposal to build a pier close to Mingary Castle. The landowner, Mr Fergusson, offered land for the purpose without compensation, including an access road into the village. It took a further five years of negotiation and fund raising, however, before the pier was eventually constructed. Once the celebrations had died down the villagers were to experience further frustration. The steamer company, MacBrayne's, refused to use the new pier saying that the approach was too shallow and dangerous rocks intervened. The owner of the local ferry, who had a contract with the company for unloading from the anchorage, supported this view. The villagers were incensed. They had seen other steamers calling at the pier to load sheep and cattle without any trouble and decided to invite other steamship companies to take their trade. In fairness it should be said that MacBrayne's main argument was that the passage to the pier was safe only at high tide which made a regular service of the kind which they operated throughout the Highlands impossible. Although unscheduled vessels used it continuously, it was not until the 1950s that MacBrayne's produced a vessel suitable for use at Mingary pier at all states of the tide and even today there is great controversy over the reduction of services during the winter months.

For nearly 150 years the main supplier of goods in the area has been the proprietor of the Ferry Stores at Kilchoan. The village shop still bears this name today. It provides the only source of petrol and diesel fuel in west Ardnamurchan.

Following tradition, the village school in Kilchoan had for long been used for community functions, meetings, weddings and celebrations of all kinds. In 1904 the local Minister proposed to the School Board that the school building should no longer be used for such purposes. His suggestion was upheld and the parishioners thereafter found themselves obliged to hold all their activities in their own homes. Determined to acquire suitable premises where such functions could be held, the villagers set about raising the necessary money. This was no mean task during the depression years of the 1920s but eventually with the help of a handsome donation from the landowner, Kenneth

M. Clark, they opened their own village hall in 1930. Today this is a centre of activity for the entire area and a place where even the most isolated families can enjoy the company of their friends.

While talented parishioners of all kinds have emerged from these spontaneous entertainments over the years, arguably the greatest bard to emerge from Ardnamurchan was Alasdair MacMhaighstir Alasdair, who was born at Dalilea on Loch Shiel in 1700. After joining the Society for the Promulgation of Christian Knowledge in 1729, he opened a village school at Kilmory where there were some forty children in need of education. A staunch supporter of the Jacobite cause, Alasdair joined Prince Charles on his march south and following the defeat at Culloden he lost his appointment as teacher in Ardnamurchan and retired to Canna from where he published his collected poems in 1751.

On the borders of Ardnamurchan with the parish of Moidart is the village of Acharacle. The name is taken from the Gaelic Ath Thorcail or Torquil's ford and it commemorates a Norse warrior who fell in battle at the ford across the river at the head of Loch Shiel.

Acharacle can be easily approached from the sea from Loch Moidart and thence across a narrow strip of land. Standing at the head of Loch Shiel, an imposing waterway by which vessels may travel many miles inland, it has been an ideal site for a settlement since prehistory. The presence of Castle Tioram a few kilometres to the north must also have been a significant factor in the development of a village on this spot.

In the sixth century St Columba visited Loch Shiel and soon after St Fhianain gave his name to an island in the loch and to the glen at its landward end, Glen Finnan. This became the seat of the priests of Ardnamurchan although the main place of worship was at Kilchoan in the west.

Castle Tioram, built in the thirteenth century, has stood the test of time remarkably well. It is built upon an island in Loch Moidart which is approachable only at low tide. The name Caisteal Tiorum (dry island) refers to the lack of fresh water which must have created some problems in time of siege. It is said that the castle was built under the instruction of Annie Nic Ruairi, the wife of John of Islay, Lord of the Isles, early in the thirteenth century. By dint of their extraordinary sea power, Macdonalds controlled most of the outer islands and much of mainland Argyll. For nearly 500 years Castle

Shiel Bridge, built 1790s (*Author's Collection*)

Tioram was the administrative centre, controlled by the Macdonalds of Clanranald. A period of fierce fighting for supremacy over the Vikings was eventually ended by treaty and marriages of convenience. A long and peaceful period of joint ownership by the Clan Macdonald, Lords of the Isles, and their Norse relations, followed. Feasting and music, poetry and song are associated with the castle during the sixteenth and seventeenth centuries but because of their strict allegiance to Roman Catholicism, following the execution of Charles I, the clan became disaffected with the Crown and, as a consequence of their involvement in the Jacobite Risings of 1715 and 1745, their lands were forfeited.

For many centuries Loch Shiel was an artery for trade and transport across a very difficult terrain and the village at the seaward end assumed great importance. Freight piers at Salen a few kilometres to the south and at Kinlochmoidart connected this inland waterway by sea with ports in the south. In 1745 Prince Charles Edward Stewart landed in Loch Moidart and sailed up Loch Shiel from Dalilea to Glen Finnan where he raised his standard. When in the late nineteenth century a railway line was laid between Fort William and Mallaig, a steamer service was introduced on the loch to connect settlements on Ardnamurchan with the rail service. Until the roads were improved and buses introduced in the 1950s, this was the main inland route in

Black house at Mingary (*Author's Collection*)

and out of the district. In recent years a regular boat service has been reintroduced to carry visitors to the Glenfinnan memorial and visitor centre at the far end of the loch.

In an attempt to improve communications and to pacify the Highlanders following the Rising of 1745, a military road was constructed linking Corran ferry (on Loch Linnhe) with Kinlochmoidart. This involved the construction of two major bridges over the River Shiel and at Ardmolich. Built to a design by Thomas Telford, the Shiel Bridge still carries traffic today while that at Ardmolich was bypassed only when the main road was carried through to Glenuig and Lochailort.

Today Acharacle is a thriving community which has retained the appearance of a crofting village, the houses each with their own parcel of land, dotted evenly across the valley floor. The crofts still function, either growing grain or vegetable crops or as grazing for sheep and cattle.

The original black houses were thatched, usually with heather, and had no windows. A hole in the roof allowed the egress of smoke from the fire whose hearth was usually in the middle of the floor. Some black houses were dived into two parts, one for the family and the other to house the stock in winter. Most of these buildings have now been replaced by twentieth-century bungalows or restored to modern standards of heating and ventilation. One of the original buildings still exists on the road out of the village, a kilometre or so beyond the Shiel Bridge at the township of Mingary.

A number of the larger village houses are villas of the Victorian era. The present hotel, which stands on the site of a much earlier coaching inn or maybe a drovers' stance, appears to have been built with nineteenth-century sporting gentlemen in mind – those who came to fish the lochs and streams for salmon and trout and to hunt for deer and game birds across the hillsides. The title of the Gillie's Restaurant tends to confirm this impression.

The nineteenth-century village church stands almost hidden by trees at the northern end of the village. This was one of the parliamentary churches which were built throughout Argyll during the 1820s and 1830s, to a similar plan devised by Thomas Telford. At the disruption of 1843 the local inhabitants to a man withdrew from the Church of Scotland in favour of the Free Church and a new church building and manse were erected at that time.

In 1900 the heritor provided another Church of Scotland building to mark the reuniting of the various breakaway groups. This is a prominent structure standing on raised ground close to the earlier church. The Free Church members, determined to retain their individual status, continue to hold regular meetings in their own church in the centre of the village.

In medieval times the Kingdom of Scotland was divided up between the great lords, chieftains of the major clans. Each laird controlled a vast territory which required an army of men, ready at all times to defend it. These private armies consisted in the main of members of the laird's own clan together with their relations by marriage and their servants. In order to ensure the loyalty of his men and so that they might at all times be at hand when most required, the laird provided every soldier with a parcel of land, to be worked by himself and his family. Although the private armies were disbanded by law following the Jacobite Rising of 1745, the system of crofting has continued and the medieval rules which govern it are largely still in place to this day.

Until the middle of the twentieth century the main occupation of the village of Salen on Loch Sunart was crofting. A glance at the Ordnance Survey map for the area shows clearly how the land has been divided up into equal-sized sections, each with its croft house.

On the croft, each household grew crops for its own consumption or for barter, as well as fodder for the beasts. Few cash payments ever changed hands: rent was paid in crops or in hours worked on the laird's estate.

A crofter was often allocated in addition, a stretch of shoreline from which he might gather seaweed for fertiliser and shellfish such as mussels and winkles for his own consumption or for sale. In the 1960s winkles fetched £1.50 for a bag sold in the East End of London. By the 1970s the price had risen to around £8.00. Today the demand for Ardnamurchan shellfish is so great that as much as £18 can be had for a bag of winkles. Whereas king prawns and scallops were once fit only to enliven the crofter's broth, today everything caught is immediately packed in ice and exported to Europe.

Common grazing for a limited number of sheep and cattle was allowed on the rough pasture of the hillsides. To ensure that there were no arguments concerning ownership of beasts or allocation of land the crofters appointed from their number a committee to make the rules and a clerk to ensure the rules were obeyed.

During the Second World War there was an influx of military personnel into the area around Salen and some of the more remote areas were cleared of civilians so that exercises and training of a most secret nature might be carried out. It was in these mountains that the Commandos practised many of their most daring exploits and it was here that coastal invasions were perfected. In the deep sea lochs merchant vessels gathered before setting out on those perilous trips in convoy, across a U-boat infested ocean.

Even in this apparently safe haven there were wartime experiences which have found their place in the history and folklore of the region. A USAF Catalina flying boat managed to attack and hole a buoy which is still displayed on Salen jetty. Three aircraft crashed on the peninsula, two of them on Sanna beach. One of these was carrying a load of rifles and ammunition which, although eventually returned to the Ministry of Defence, were said firstly to have contributed handsomely to the inhabitant's meagre wartime rations. It seems that venison appeared on the menu of most of the surrounding villages for some weeks!

The presence of troops brought a certain amount of trade to the villages and widened the outlook of the local people. There were marriages which were to bring some servicemen back to live here permanently after the war while Ardnamurchan girls went away to join their husbands' families. The two world wars had other less agreeable effects. The tradition of bearing arms lies deep in the heart of every Highlander and in Ardnamurchan every tiny township has its war memorial, weighted down by a disproportionate number of names of the fallen, many from the same family.

During the 1950s and '60s, at a time of increasing affluence elsewhere in Britain, it is hardly surprising that the people of the peninsula, having found it impossible to obtain a comparable standard of living on their crofts, began to drift away into the towns or took up offers of emigration and a better life overseas. Many turned again to the Forestry Commission for seasonal employment which fitted in well with crofting. The technology used today in the harvesting and replanting of woodlands demands far less manpower than in former times but both men and women are employed in preparing and maintaining the forest paths, in husbanding the nature reserves and in acting as guides and forest rangers.

By the 1960s the tourist industry was providing a valuable addition to the district's economy. In Salen there were already two hotels and a number of boarding houses providing accommodation for visitors. Disused cottages were refurbished and let by the week as self-catering establishments.

Salen was one of the first places on the peninsula to have a supply of electricity. In 1928 the local landowner, Kenneth M. Clark, installed a generating plant at his Gorten estate, sufficient to supply a limited amount of electricity to the entire village. It was not until the 1980s, however, when the Scottish Hydro-Electricity Board took over responsibility for the public supply to the entire peninsula, that residents could claim to be fully electrified to twentieth-century standards. Even today there are isolated dwellings which remain without electric power other than that provided by a small domestic generator.

Until the 1960s villages such Salen were virtually self-sufficient for normal everyday requirements. According to the *Third Statistical Account* (1961), the village still had its mason, carpenter, blacksmith, shoemaker and tailor. It is unlikely one will find a tailor or shoemaker in situ today. There will always be a call for certain local services such as the building and motor trades but these tend to be carried out by the general handyman who may one day replace slates on a roof and the next be cutting grass or building a dry-stone wall. Generally, skilled craftsmen are obliged to go to the larger towns and cities if they are to make a proper living and it is to the towns that the rural population now looks for such services.

The principal village of Ardnamurchan, regarded today as the centre of the region, is Strontian which lies at the head of Loch Sunart. It is the least typical of the Ardnamurchan villages because of its long association with industries of the Industrial Revolution, an event which had little or no impact upon the remainder of the area.

Lead was discovered here early in the eighteenth century. The York Buildings Company acquired from the heritor, the Duke of Argyll, a lease to extract and process the ore. The company opened up mines in various locations along the hill road between Strontian and Polloch and installed the necessary industrial plant. It also provided housing for the workers, most of whom had to be brought in from elsewhere to operate the mines. Eventually a string of small villages grew up around the mine entrances; the townships of Anaheilt, Scotstown and Ariundle indicate the line of the main mineral-bearing seam and were known collectively as New York.

At the village of Strontian itself, a barracks was built in timber to accommodate the mine manager and the original workforce. As individual housing became available, the occupants moved out and in 1730 this wooden building became the London Inn. It was eventually replaced by a stone building, and there has been an inn of one sort or another on the site ever since. A fine stone house of similar date was built on an adjacent site to accommodate the mine manager and his family. With extensions and alterations this is now the Loch Sunart Hotel. The smelter which produced the ingots of lead was conveniently situated within the village. Its stone outer walls were retained when the post office replaced it on the same site.

When after ten years their lease expired, the York Buildings Company did not renew it. The Duke of Argyll, who had had shares in the original enterprise, now took control of the operation himself.

At the height of their productivity, the Strontian mines were exporting 600 tons of lead annually. In 1753, sixty tons were incorporated in the roofing of the new Inverary Castle. The Napoleonic Wars kept the lead mines at maximum productivity, much of the lead shot used in the fighting having been produced here. After hostilities ended, however, demand for lead began to fall away. At about the same time, the men encountered poor seams, which proved difficult to mine economically. Production costs rose alarmingly resulting in the closure of all the mines by 1871.

In 1764 the geologist, Thomas Hope, while working in the locality, recognised a hitherto unknown mineral occurring in association with the lead. He named his find Stronianite, after the village in which he was staying. It was not until 1808, however, that Sir Humphry Davy, using an electrolytic process, successfully isolated the element Strontium from Strontianite. The extraction of a hitherto unknown element gave rise to a certain amount of speculation on the London Stock Market but at that time the only use to be found for strontium was in the production of red-coloured fireworks so the speculators soon lost interest. Today the element is an important component of the electronics industry as well as being used extensively in industrial processes and in medical science in the form of a radioactive isotope.

In 1904 an attempt was made to reopen the lead mines but the payload proved to be uneconomical. Again, in the 1950s, the nuclear power industry created increased demands for lead and as a consequence further surveys were carried out. There was sporadic prospecting for a time but the only commercial outcome of all this activity has been the recovery of the mineral barytes from the spoil heaps.

Towards the end of the twentieth century, developments associated with drilling for North Sea oil created a demand for barytes, a mineral important in the manufacture of a special mud used as a lubricant in deep sea drilling. Barytes is composed of the sulphate and carbonate of barium and is found in close association with the ores of metals such as lead and zinc. It is commonly found in the spoil associated with lead mines. The waste tips of the Strontian mines have in recent years provided a rich harvest of this material.

Remnants of a once-flourishing industry are still recognisable alongside the road from Strontian to Polloch. Other mines, where the buildings are better preserved, are situated well up in the glens and accessible only on foot.

There had at one time been 500 men employed in the production of lead. With the closure of the mines towards the end of the nineteenth century, there was a general exodus of families from the district, leaving behind only a small, ageing village population. The only viable industry by this time was charcoal burning to supply the iron foundries at Bonawe and Furnace but these too were soon to

Lead mines at Strontian (*Author's Collection*)

close. The glens converging upon Loch Sunart, heavily denuded of their hardwood trees, were to wait a further hundred years before replanting began.

Other work had to be found. From the burgeoning steel industry of Lanarkshire came a demand for birch brooms for sweeping the casting floors. Those ancient birch woods, which had been carefully coppiced by the charcoal burners, proved ideal for the purpose and local people were engaged in the manufacture of brooms until the collapse of the steel industry in the latter part of the twentieth century.

In Ardnamurchan and Morvern the Presbyterian influence was always very strong and when, after the Disruption of 1843, the disaffected minister of Strontian resigned his living, many members of his congregation united in his support.

In 1843 the patrons of the Strontian church were a family called Riddell, staunch Episcopalians who were totally opposed to the Disruption. When members of the breakaway Free Church approached Riddell for a piece of land upon which to build a new meeting place for their worship, the request was refused. Undaunted, the congregation collected sufficient funds to approach a Glasgow boatbuilder for a vessel suitable for use as a floating church. This was moored on Loch Sunart, close by the village and for some time services were regularly held on board. During one violent storm, the vessel broke away from its moorings and was cast up upon the beach. As the shore between High and Low water was Crown property and not belonging to the Riddell family, the church boat was made fast on the beach and continued in use. Eventually Riddell relented and granted the Free Church members a parcel of ground close to the shore where they built the church and manse which are still in use today.

There had been schools on the peninsula for centuries, beginning with those set up by the Irish missionaries, and by the eighteenth century many children had access to some form of schooling, provided either by the parish or through the auspices of the Edinburgh Society for the Promulgation of Christian Knowledge. In the more remote areas, however, children worked on the crofts and what little education they received came from friends and family. There was generally a Sabbath school available, however, where Bible teaching incorporated the fundamentals of reading and writing. In 1945 when many small schools closed for lack of pupils, Strontian became the centre for education in the parish.

Until the 1944 Education Act compelled all local authorities to provide secondary education for pupils under the age of fifteen, only the very brightest children and those of the more affluent families attended secondary school in Oban. When Ardnamurchan and Morvern were taken into the Highland Region in 1976, secondary schooling was provided at Fort William High School but for the young people of the peninsula the journey was no less arduous.

In 2003 Ardnamurchan Community College was opened in Strontian, providing education not only for the eleven- to eighteen-year-olds, but also offering opportunities for Further Education for adults. This facility, which is provided with computer links with the University of the Highlands centred in Inverness, has opened up the possibility of advanced education for all, no matter what their former schooling or how remote their location.

The Forestry Commision's decision to begin a major planting programme in Glen Strontian in the 1940s did much to halt the flow of people out of the area. Since then the number of permanent residents has changed very little. Today the village of Strontian can claim to be the largest settlement in Ardnamurchan having a number of shops, a pub and a hotel, a post office and tourist centre as well as the new Community College. Private motoring has made daily commuting to the industrial and commercial centre of Fort William a viable possibility. Many people are now able to live in the country and work in the town and there is a demand for good-quality housing around Strontian.

The original village buildings which could be saved have been renovated in recent years either for permanent residence or as holiday homes. To the north of the village green is a substantial new housing scheme which blends pleasingly with the remainder of the buildings. Such developments, however, are strictly limited by planning regulations.

The uniquely wild nature of the area is being jealously guarded for there are very few such places left for the enjoyment of the nation as a whole. In order to preserve the natural heritage while at the same time improving public awareness of the countryside, the Forestry Commission, in collaboration with Scottish Natural Heritage and other organisations, has made strenuous efforts in recent years to improve accessibility for the general public. Such activity requires the input of a fully employed, well-informed workforce. Who better than those who have lived in the region all their lives to undertake this work?

While Ardnamurchan, although sparsely populated, can claim a network of villages, its neighbouring parish of Morvern, which occupies the southern of the two peninsulas, has only one settlement remaining, deserving of the name. Lochaline lies on the south coast opposite the island of Mull with which it enjoys a regular ferry connection.

The Morvern peninsula is almost bisected by a low valley which runs SE/NW for eleven miles from Loch Aline to Loch Teacuis. Only seventy feet above sea level, this valley receives a watershed from the heights on either side which rise in some cases to above 600 m. On the north coast just offshore in Loch Sunart lie the islands of Oronsay and Carna. Originally most of Morvern belonged to the Macleans of Duart and Morvern, whose stronghold was Kinlochaline at the mouth of the River Aline. The entire peninsula fell into the hands of the Campbells during the seventeenth century. Not until 1912 did the Macleans regain possession by purchasing the land from the Argyll Estate. The Macdonalds also owned territory here, building a number of castles along the coast, the chief of which is at Ardtornish.

At one time there were extensive settlements along the north coast and in the valley of the Aline where the soil was fertile and crofting was the way of life. The clearances of the nineteenth century had a disastrous effect upon the population for, unlike Ardnamurchan, where crofters were removed to other parts of the parish, here there was no alternative to emigration. Many people went overseas, others sought work in the cities. In 1831 there had been over 2,000 inhabitants in the parish. By 1881 the population had fallen to less than 1,000 and in 1951 there were only 460 people remaining. The numbers stayed steady during the second half of the twentieth century and the ownership of second homes and the popularity of self-catering accommodation have led in recent years to the reinstatement of a number of discarded cottages. Four miles from Lochaline the abandoned village of Inniemore disappeared under planting by the Forestry Commission in the 1930s. When felling took place in the 1990s the village again came to light. Twenty-two houses, seven corn-drying kilns, four walled kale gardens and a mill, all in a good state of preservation, were discovered.

At one time each half of the parish had its own parish church, Kiluintag in the western part and a second church close to Lochaline village, dedicated to St Columba, at Kiel. A nine-foot-high stone cross dating from the fifteenth century stands before the Kiel church which enjoys a magnificent view across the Sound of Mull. According to the 1951 *Statistical Account*, services were still held regularly at Kiel church and at the township of Ferinish, while occasional services were held in schools at Kinloch and Claggan. Today all such activity centres upon Lochaline.

Morvern boasts some of the most extensive deposits of white sand anywhere in the British Isles and is an important source of supply to the glass-making industry. The sand-quarrying company has for long been a major employer in the area and was responsible for bringing electric power to the district soon after the Second World War. The sand quarries also brought new blood into the area when, after the war, workers were introduced from Europe's hordes of displaced persons. A temporary village of twenty-five wooden houses was erected at Kiel to accommodate the incomers. For a while the population figures were more encouraging but fell off again as mechanisation replaced the workforce. Sandstone is still taken from the cliffs above Loch Aline and transported to the crushing plant beside the pier by a private railway line.

Until improvements were made to the road in the latter part of the twentieth century all communication with the parish took place by sea. So difficult is the terrain along the coast that one of the most substantial employers in Morvern, the stone quarrying which takes place at Glensanda, is inaccessible to local people, the workforce being ferried across Loch Linnhe from Appin and Ballachulish.

In the 1950s the main occupation was still farming. Land west of Lochaline came into public ownership before 1939 and the Department of Agriculture lets a number of coastal crofts to tenants. More crofts are worked at Bunavullin where the owners are obliged to subsidise their living by undertaking additional employment. Cattle and sheep, including dairy cattle, are raised along the valley floor and on the surrounding hills but the main crops on the crofts in 1951 were potatoes, turnips, oats and hay. Today many crofters have diversified to supply a more demanding public market. Cheap polythene growing tunnels and the introduction of silage to replace hay as winter fodder have gone some way to relieving the crofter from the tyranny of the weather.

From the 1920s the Forestry Commission has been another major employer and today is heavily engaged in the establishment of facilities for tourists which should eventually match those of Ardnamurchan.

Despite its isolation the community centred upon Lochaline enjoys a robust social life. While there is plenty of room for improvement of facilities for both residents and tourists the magnificent scenery and copious wildlife of the area is compensation enough for the enthusiastic naturalist.

The parish of Ardgour is a narrow strip of country approximately 8 km wide and 32 km long, bordering on the old county boundary with Inverness to the north and with the parish boundary with Morvern in the south. It is a mountainous region along the shores of Loch Linnhe where there is little room for settlement of any kind. The Ardgour Estate is the principal land owner, farming sheep and cattle. There is little opportunity for arable farming. The other three estates are principally concerned with providing sporting opportunities on a commercial basis. What few crofts remain tend to support a greater population than do the large estates which, in these technological times, can operate on a minimum of staff.

The village of Ardgour with its landing for the Connel ferry, serves as a lifeline to the people of all three parishes. With its single inn, no doubt standing upon the site of a number of predecessors, it is little more than a row of houses and industrial shelters crammed up tight against a solid wall of rock leaving just sufficient room for the road which has to cater for increasingly heavy traffic. The pier at Ardgour, built and formerly owned by the Ardgour Estate is now, together with the ferry, the responsibility of the Highlands and

Islands Development Board. The ferry, which is large enough to carry about twenty-four vehicles as well as pedestrians, is the quickest means of travelling between Fort William and Oban and the villages of the largely untamed country to the north.

10

GLENCOE AND BALLACHULISH

More slate, Viking invaders and an infamous massacre

Loch Leven marks the natural boundary of Argyll in the north yet for centuries, until the regionalisation of Scotland in the 1970s, the lands lying below the southern slopes of the Ben Nevis range were also incorporated within the county. Included in this account, therefore, are the villages of North Ballachulish and Kinlochleven and the estate of Mamore together with South Ballachullish and the village of Glencoe.

The sheltered waters of Loch Leven and its ready access to the inner isles first attracted Neolithic man to the site more than 6,000 years ago. Early settlements were established upon islands in the loch or on crannogs. The glen, the bleak moorland and forests beyond were places where a man could be taken by the beasts or sucked down into a bog and the nature of his disappearance would remain forever a mystery. It is little wonder therefore that, like the majority of the tribes in Scotland, the people of the glen believed strongly in a malevolent spirit world which must be appeased. A reverence for special wells, trees and stones lives on in the customs of the Highlander. The habit of placing an iron object beside the baby's cradle to keep away the fairies is still practised in the Highlands today. It is dangerous to damage a forest tree in case one disturbs the fairy within and everyone is aware of the necessity of planting a rowan tree beside the house to keep away the evil spirits. Although few today would confess to a belief in the presence of kelpies or water-horses, those strange creatures who lure the unsuspecting traveller to his death with their bridles of precious stones, it is a brave Scot who will pass by a well without throwing in a few coins for luck! The mysticism of Glen Coe and the village of Glencoe at its western end is illustrated by the tales arising from the work of one of Scotland's earliest poets, the famous Ossian.

The life of the poet himself is shrouded in magic and mystery: Ossian was the son of Fionn MacCumhail, the founder of the Clan Macdonald, and from early childhood he listened to the Celtic legends of his tribe. An accomplished minstrel, he composed poems and music describing the beauties of his natural surroundings and the history of his people. The legends he sang of often spoke of Tir-nan-Og, the island of eternal youth, a place he longed to visit.

It is said that one evening, as Ossian sat upon the shore he was overheard singing by Niamh, daughter of Manannan MacLir, the ruler of Tir-nan-Og. Niamh fell instantly in love with the young mortal and spirited him away to Tir-nan-Og where she held him captive for 300 years. Quite unaware of the passage of time, Ossian remained unchanged throughout his stay. At last he felt the urge to visit his home and mortal friends once again. Niamh gave him a fleet-footed white stallion to carry him swiftly on his journey insisting he return as soon as possible. As he was leaving she warned him that should he actually set one foot upon the ground of his homeland, he would never be able to return to Tir-nan-Og. Unfortunately, while the poet himself had survived for 300 years without a change in his appearance, his friends and family had not. In his grief at finding them dead and gone, Ossian slid from his horse and fell to the ground, weeping. As his foot touched the soil of Alba, the fairy horse disappeared and the minstrel instantly changed from a handsome youth to a wizened old man. Blind, alone and helpless, he sought shelter in a cave where he spent the remainder of his life writing poetry about his lost paradise of Tir-nan-Og.

High on the face of Aonach Dubh, the great shoulder of Bidean nam Bheinn, overlooking Glen Coe, one may find the cave in which, it is believed, he spent his final years. His work traversed the centuries, related in the Gaelic tongue from father to son through the generations. At last the words were written down in the Gaelic language and eventually, during the eighteenth century, translated into English.

In his *Journey Through England and Scotland 1784*, St Fond the French geologist recalls his meeting with a Dalmally schoolmaster, Patrick Fraser, who claimed possession of fragments of Ossian's work written in the Gaelic, which he was attempting to translate into English. The Edinburgh scholar James MacPherson spent much of his life tracking down and translating fragments of the ancient poet's work. One reason for Dr Johnson's visit to the Highlands in 1773 was to find traces of Ossian's poetry. Sadly, he returned to England, empty-handed.

Among the oldest sites of human habitation in Loch Leven is a tiny islet, Eilean Munde, which has served the population of the glen as a

Eilean Munde Parish Church in Loch Leven (*Author's Collection*)

burial site, probably since the coming of Irish missionaries in the sixth century. At one time the church, the ruins of which still survive at the northern end of the island, served as the parish church of Elanmunde, a parish comprising the settlements on the north shore of Loch Leven in the districts of Mamore and Onich and on the southern shore, Glencoe and parts of Appin. This parish was subsumed at some time during the seventeenth century when the north part became a part of Inverness-shire and the south became joined with Lismore and Appin. While the burial ground continued in use, the church was made redundant in 1653 and quickly fell into ruin.

Within the churchyard can be found a number of medieval monuments carved in the style of the Iona School. Here too can be seen the burial enclosure of the Macdonalds and a division of the clan known as the McIans of Glencoe. Among them is the tomb of the MacIan Chieftain whose failure, in February 1692, to arrive in time to swear an oath of allegiance to King William, was the alleged cause of the Glencoe massacre.

Two centuries on from the arrival of the Irish priests on the west coast of Argyll, the Vikings came to plunder, pillage and rape, but also to fall in love and settle down, adding the Norseman's genes to the Highland pool. Loch Leven, with its deep water and steep-sided hills, must surely have reminded the Vikings of their own fjords at home. With them, the invaders brought their own gods, their customs and their culture. Skilled in boat-building and in the use of iron, they were to add handsomely to the colourful pattern of life in these remote parts. The Viking invaders are remembered in the place-names of the district: Clach Phadruig or Peter's Rock below the Ballachulish Bridge is said to be the place from which a Viking warrior attempted unsuccessfully to save his drowning son. A bay is called Camus Thorsta – Thorsta's bay, definitely of Viking origin, and a second is named after Fridaig, a Norse goddess.

The bay beside which the village of Ballachullish developed, Bishop's Bay, was particularly favoured by the Vikings. Here there was excellent shelter for their boats. There was an easily defended place on shore in which to store their supplies and from which to send out forays into the surrounding countryside. Legend has it that a great battle was fought between Fionn MacCumhail, the founder of Clan Macdonald and the Viking, Earagen, King of Lochlann. Earagen sailed his forty Viking ships into the mouth of Loch Leven and landed at West Laroch on the shores of the loch. Having made a raid on nearby villages and crofts, the Vikings were celebrating their victory by feasting on the shore. Once they had been thoroughly wined and dined, a party of local tribesmen descended upon the drunken horde, taking them completely by surprise; 105 Vikings lost their lives in the skirmish and the rivers, it is said, ran red with blood. Enormous cairns nearby, placed over the massed graves, are testimony to the numbers of men slain. According to all accounts, after that there were no further Viking raids in the area!

At the mouth of Loch Leven stands the village of Ballachulish once noted only for the ferry which linked Lochaber with the land of Lorn. Today it owes its fame to the slate rock which forms the steep hillside at its back. Until the opening of the quarries late in the seventeenth century, the township consisted of a few houses and crofts which had grown up around a drover's stance and the ferry landing.

It is said that it was men from Easdale who first reported the valuable slate rock of Ballachulish. Returning home through the pass of Glen Coe after working the quarries at Aberfeldy, they recognised the distinctive blue-grey slate with its crystals of iron pyrites and described the outcrop to their masters. The Easdale slate belt lies along the geological fault line which produced the Great Glen and outcrops of similar slate rock can be found from Jura, north-eastwards to Inverness.

Slate was first taken from this location in 1693 when the West Quarry (West Laroch) was opened. The slate beds here occur high

Ballachulish slate quarry, 1880s (*Easdale Museum*)

up on the hillside and it was possible to take out the rock using a step method of extraction without the need to pump the diggings dry. Here the wooden wedges used to split the rock had water thrown over them to make them swell and force the rock apart. The large chunks of rock which were cut out could be hauled free and sent down the slope on a sledge for splitting and cutting into suitable sizes for roofing tiles.

In the course of the next 150 years the output of slates increased year by year until in the 1850s the annual output was between 5–7 million slates, produced by a workforce of some 300 men, women and children. In this labour-intensive industry, work could be found for every able-bodied soul in the village.

When work began in the late seventeenth century it was men from Cumberland and from Easdale who worked the slate, but as local men began to acquire the skills of the trade they took over from the incomers. By the time the 1841 *Statistical Account* was prepared it was reported that all the quarry workers were local people whose common language was Gaelic.

Groups of cottages at both West and East Laroch were built to house the quarry workers. These were of the usual two-roomed variety but had in addition a byre, in which to over-winter a few beasts. Every tenant was allowed to rent a plot of land to grow his own vegetables for his family and a stretch of seashore from which he might gather seaweed for fertiliser. As the population increased, the two villages merged to form the one large settlement which today takes the name of Ballachulish. Few of the original cottages of the slate workers remain. In the seventy years since the quarries closed down, many have been replaced by larger, two-storey dwellings which are more in keeping with modern living standards.

At the peak of slate production, Ballachulish housed 587 men employed by the slate industry including blacksmiths, carpenters and other craftsmen. Originally all the slate was transported by sea, special piers being erected at both East and West Laroch to cope with the flow of exports. To begin with, the trading vessels were ocean-going sailing ships which took the slates to any port in the British Isles and across the Atlantic to Canada and the United States. By the 1840s, puffers were carrying slates via either the Caledonian Canal or Crinan Canal to the developing cities along the east coast and in the industrial heartland of Lowland Scotland. By the time the branch line of the Callander and Oban railway reached Ballachulish in 1903, the market for slated roofs was already declining to be replaced by a call for clay tiles or cheap imports of less durable slates from Spain and Portugal. The railway did little to improve business in the quarries although it did encourage tourism and provided alternatives for employment to those who were willing to commute daily to Oban.

With the decline in the slate industry, the movement of commercial shipping in and out of the loch almost ceased and the piers fell into disrepair. Only the continued presence of the ferry, which in 1912 was converted to a vehicular ferry, kept the village on the map.

In 1975 work was completed on a road bridge linking North and South Ballachulish. When this was opened, most road traffic was diverted to cross the bridge rather than take the more circuitous route through Kinlochleven which, in the days of long queues for the ferry, had been a viable alternative.

Ballachulish benefited by the increased flow of traffic and a cluster of hotels, either newly built or converted from older properties of distinction, bears witness to the increasing popularity of the village as a tourist centre.

Ballachulish car ferry, 1939 (*Dr W.M. Edgar*)

Recently, a visitor centre has been opened in the village and moves are afoot to restore one of the quarries as a working museum with the facility for producing small batches of slate for specific purposes.

During the clan wars which followed the departure of the Norsemen, the Macdonalds held Glen Coe and the lands around Loch Leven. Their township, which because of its naturally well-protected site appears never to have warranted the building of a castle, stands at the seaward end of the narrow gorge of Glen Coe.

It is difficult to believe that the peaceful village which today consists of little more than a street of mostly nineteenth- and twentieth-century houses should hold such an infamous place in the history of the Highlands or that the spectacular glen at whose mouth it sits could ever have been the scene of brutal carnage. In semi-darkness, however, as the mists roll down the hillside and the shadows lengthen, Glen Coe becomes the most threatening of all the glens in Scotland.

For centuries, Glen Coe was the easiest and shortest route to the sea from eastern Scotland, north of the River Forth. It was also the most hazardous, its steep-sided, narrow gorge being easily defended by those who claimed it as their own. The Macdonalds took a heavy toll from travellers passing through the glen; drovers paid dearly to be allowed to move their herds through to the trysts at Crieff. With little cultivable land of their own, for more than two centuries the Macdonalds and MacIans of Glen Coe made a living by stealing cattle and crops from their neighbours, in particular the Campbells of Glenorchy. They made frequent forays into Glen Orchy, even setting fire on one occasion to Achallada Castle, the seat of the Campbell chieftain. It is not surprising, therefore, that there was little love lost between the clans.

The Macdonalds, largely members of the Episcopalian church, were staunch upholders of the Jacobite cause. By supporting Montrose in his attempt to preserve the crown of Scotland and England for the deposed King James VII (II of England), they heaped upon themselves the wrath of influential members of the government in Westminster. The terrible massacre which occurred in Glencoe in the early hours of the morning of 13 February 1692 has received a great deal of attention from writers and journalists through the ages. Their accounts are frequently biased and the facts distorted or ignored to prove a point. The accused are the English, occasionally King Billy himself, and most frequently, the Campbells. Few of the brief accounts of the tragedy one reads in the guidebooks ever mention the real villain of the piece, Sir John Dalrymple, the Master of Stair and Secretary of State for Scotland.

In an attempt to pacify the Highlands following the defeat of Montrose, King William III agreed to grant amnesty to any clan chieftain who would proclaim a solemn oath of allegiance to his sovereign. The date of 31 December 1691 was chosen as the deadline by which the clans must swear allegiance to the Crown, and loyal dignitaries were appointed in various parts of the Highlands to administer the oath. A number of the Jacobite supporters felt bound to obtain the permission of their exiled 'king' before taking the oath and waited until late into the year for his message of approval. James dithered so long that by the time MacIan of Glencoe received word from him, it was already midwinter. Old and sick as he was, in order to save his clansmen from the wrath of King Billy, MacIan determined to journey on foot across the Nevis range to Inverlochy, to take the oath. There was treachery afoot even at this stage in the affair, for it was only when MacIan had arrived in Inverlochy that he was informed he must take the oath at the County seat of the Duke of Argyll, in Inveraray! Through the ice and snow of midwinter, the old chieftain made the perilous journey back across the mountains to Inveraray, arriving only just in time to meet the deadline on Old Year's Night.

Unfortunately, the Sheriff was away from home, celebrating the New Year with his friends and family and did not return for some days. When he did at last arrive, he accepted that MacIan's intentions had been proper and agreed to administer the oath. Alas for MacIan, an informer had already conveyed the news to Dalrymple that MacIan had failed to take the oath by the set time. At Westminster, it had been agreed that, as a warning to the rest, an example should be made of one of the dissenting Highland chieftains and Dalrymple had already decided that the Macdonalds would be the chosen clan. Dalrymple ordered that the entire population of Glencoe under the age of seventy be wiped out. The troops chosen to carry out the sentence were from the Earl of Argyle's Regiment under the command of General Sir Thomas Livingston who was stationed at Inverlochy.

The fact that there were so many Campbells amongst the troops chosen for the task was a matter of chance rather than design. The massacre which ensued was not, as many have suggested, revenge taken by one clan upon another, but the action of an army of regular troops obeying the directive of their Commander in Chief who was Dalrymple, the Master of Stair. There is little doubt, however, that the choice of Robert Campbell of Glen Lyon to lead the two companies of men who were to carry out the task was quite intentional. Campbell was a discredited army officer who had lost all his family's wealth and taken to alcohol as an escape from his misfortunes. No matter what amount of compassion might have stayed his hand, he could not afford to cross his superiors, in particular Dalrymple, to whom he was heavily in debt.

The plan was for two companies of the king's troops to go to Glencoe where they would be billeted for some days with the villagers. A third company was camped at the western end of the glen, blocking any escape by way of Loch Leven while a forth company of soldiers was to cross the mountains from Inverlochy to block the eastern end of the pass.

Their chief having already taken the oath, the villagers believed themselves quite safe from further reprisals and, while wary of the presence of troops in the village, nevertheless showed them their accustomed Highland hospitality. It is believed that some of the soldiers, not wishing to abuse the kindness of their hosts, warned

The solitary grandeur of Glen Coe (*Author's Collection*)

them of the intended treachery and allowed them to escape the village before the signal was given to attack. The order to begin the slaughter was given shortly before dawn on 13 February 1692. There followed a scene of fearful butchery and chaos but when the work was done, it was discovered that all but 38 of the 500 Macdonalds in the glen had fled into the mountains. The dead included the chief, MacIan, and his immediate family.

In the midwinter snow and ice, with biting cold winds swirling around the mountaintops, it was impossible to tell how many of the Macdonalds perished of exposure during the night. Almost certainly it was a greater number than those who had been butchered in their beds. The military plan had, nevertheless, been doubly thwarted for not only did many of the villagers escape the massacre but the troops crossing the mountains from Inverlochy, hampered by the weather, failed to arrive at the eastern end of the pass. Those of the Macdonalds who survived the night were able to escape to the comparative safety of Glen Orchy and Glen Creran where, despite animosity between the two clans, they were taken in and sheltered by Campbell families.

So much pain and death has left its mark upon the narrow glen. Although the massacre itself took place in the village at the far end of the pass, one cannot ignore a feeling of overwhelming despair as one wanders beside the stream or climbs the mist-shrouded slopes in the wake of those panic-stricken villagers, fleeing for their lives. There have been other massacres, just as bloody, often of larger numbers, but the real infamy of Glencoe lay in the abuse of traditional Highland hospitality. It is the manner in which the soldiers accepted bed and board, making merry amongst these simple village folk, before turning upon them so viciously, which has marked the Glencoe massacre as one of the most terrible events in Scottish history.

Since all the houses were put to the torch by soldiers, very little remains of the original village. For long, Glencoe lay in ruins. The survivors, reluctant to return to their homes, went to the Lowlands to find work or joined the increasing numbers of Highlanders seeking a different way of life in the Americas. During the eighteenth and early nineteenth centuries nothing was done to encourage reoccupation. This was a time when landowners were desirous of clearing the land for sheep. They were not about to reconstruct a settlement when so many others were being laid to waste.

Only one house of eighteenth-century origin remains. Its roof construction, recently re-thatched with heather, suggests a date prior to the general resurgence which took place within the village in the mid nineteenth century. In recent years this particular building has been converted into a small museum. The later houses, which are positioned along either side of the village street are built to a pattern of working men's cottages common throughout the Highlands in the 1850s and '60s. Larger buildings of two storeys and with several public rooms, were built towards the end of the nineteenth century when tourism was beginning to develop and the provision of bed and breakfast for visitors became an acceptable way of making a living. When, in the latter part of the twentieth century, a bypass was constructed around the village, income from passing traffic was seriously depleted. A new Visitor Centre, opened in May 2002, stands beside the main road outwith the village. Visited annually by thousands of tourists, it does little to encourage visitors into Glencoe village and has had scarcely any impact upon the local economy.

The National Trust for Scotland in 1935 acquired the land between Glen Coe and Glen Etive and in 1937 that between Glen Coe and Loch Leven. In the intervening years further areas have been acquired so that most of the land is now owned for the nation. While this is excellent news for the visitors it does not provide for a great deal

Glencoe Museum (*Author's Collection*)

of employment for the local population. There is a singular lack of cattle in the lower pastures although sheep still graze the hillsides. Here and there in the glen the presence of a solitary but and ben with smoke rising from its chimney suggests the existence of a shepherd and his family. The demise of the slate industry and the closure of the aluminium works at Kinlochleven must have had their effect upon this village as well as others around the shores of Loch Leven. While a few residents are engaged in work on the land or in the nearby forests, more choose to commute, travelling daily to Fort William or to Glensanda quarry, across Loch Linnhe.

Here, as elsewhere in the Highlands, the computer has made working from home a viable possibility and the village school benefits from being online with others scattered around the area.

It was not until the opening of the road bridge across Loch Leven in the 1970s that the village of North Ballachulish really expanded. A small township associated with the ferry is indicated by the occasional nineteenth-century house and the presence of the late nineteenth-century church. The oldest building in the village is probably the inn.

Considerable housing developments took place here in the last decades of the twentieth century. A small factory making exclusive confectionery has given employment to many of the villagers and a number of hotels and boarding houses provide for the increasing numbers of visitors in the tourist season.

The village of Kinlochleven at the head of the loch is bisected by the River Leven and lies on the boundary between Inverness-shire and Argyll. It grew, in a very short space of time, from a small township to a large village housing workers in the hydroelectric plant and aluminium-extraction works which were developed by the British Aluminium Company during the first decade of the twentieth century.

Having purchased the southern water catchments of Ben Nevis, the British Aluminium Company dammed the River Leven and created the Blackwater reservoir. This drives the turbines of a hydroelectric power station which initially provided power for the electrical process of smelting aluminium ore, bauxite, imported from Spain. The enterprise was one of a number of attempts made in the Highlands at this time to generate repopulation and to encourage other occupations which were related to providing services for the enlarged community. A new housing development in the village of Kinlochleven was built to accommodate the influx of workers to the aluminium plant. Unfortunately, the developers were concerned more with practicalities than aesthetics. The housing was of a high standard for the times with piped water, bathrooms and mains drainage, electric lighting and a form of central heating but the materials used in construction were quite inappropriate for the area and the village was regarded generally as an eyesore. This, coupled with the unsightly mounds of waste created by the aluminium-smelting process, resulted in antagonism amongst those living in the surrounding area and drew cries of disapproval from the tourists who had come to see unspoiled nature in all her wild, rare beauty.

There was no denying the benefits brought to the region by the aluminium works, however. People from Ballachulish and Glencoe, whose livelihoods were already, in 1908, threatened by a declining slate industry, found an outlet for their skills, while local businesses of all kinds discovered a ready market for their services.

The aluminium works missed an opportunity for placating the surrounding villages when they failed to extend their electricity supply beyond Kinlochleven. It was not until 1951 that electricity came to Glencoe and Ballachulish, when the villages were connected to the National Grid. The aluminium works ceased operation soon after the Second World War and the British Aluminium Company sold off its housing stock to private buyers.

Kilochleven soon had the largest population of any village in the area, warranting a school sufficient to provide junior and secondary education in addition to normal primary classes. Formerly, other village schools had provided only for children up to twelve or thirteen, only the most able pupils continuing their education at Oban High School. Now children coming to the end of their primary education could attend Kinlochleven School for their two final years, leaving at fourteen. As early as 1914, pupils were being transported from outlying parts by bus. By the time the 1951 *Statistical Account* was written there were eighty-three pupils including some from Inverness-shire. Following reorganisation of Local Government in 1975 and the subsequent changes to county boundaries which followed the dissolution of regional government in the 1990s, the villages on the north shore of Loch Leven together with the school fall within Inverness-shire.

During the First World War Kinlochleven was the site of a prisoner of war camp and it is still possible to make out the concrete footings of Nissen huts from that period.

Today the village of Kinlochleven is a dormitory housing estate for Fort William where there are a number of small engineering works providing a variety of employment. The only local employment is connected with providing services for the villagers themselves or within the tourism industry. The area is renowned for hill walking and mountain climbing, and in Glen Coe, for skiing. The introduction of a ski lift has increased the popularity of the area and has done as much as the visitor centre to encourage tourism.

11

GLENORCHY AND INISHAIL

*A hospitaller knight, an amazing dynasty of blacksmiths
and a notorious cattle rustler*

Dominated by Ben Cruachan to the west, and encircled by mountains, the parish of Glenorchy and Inishail lies within a group of sheltered valleys and is one of the few Argyll parishes which is bounded neither by the sea nor a sea loch. What it lacks in coastline, however, it makes up for in fast-running waters, inland lochs, relatively easily negotiable mountain passes and fertile pasture in the valley bottoms and on the lower slopes.

Three main river valleys divide the parish: Glen Orchy and Glen Strae run parallel to one another NE/SW while Glen Lochy runs due west from Tyndrum. The Rivers Orchy and Strae join the Lochy near Dalmally to flow together into the northern end of Loch Awe.

Attack upon Bruce and his Followers at the Pass of Brander, by Mottram – lithograph (*Author's Collection*)

The earliest settlers, around 4000 BC, lived on the numerous islets within the lochs. In Loch Awe there is evidence of crannogs in the shallows nearer the shore. In Loch Tulla to the north of the parish is one such crannog of great antiquity, still in sufficiently good condition to show how these man-made islands were constructed of boulders and tree trunks. Nomadic peoples sought shelter in caves and built cairns to commemorate their dead.

A small knoll to the south of the village of Dalmally marks the position of a Bronze Age fort or dun. This is Barachastalain. The remains are of a circular stone building some fifteen metres in diameter and they suggest a pre-Christian settlement where the village now stands.

Later visitors to the valley came not from the east but from the west, arriving by sea from Ireland and the Outer Hebrides and hauling their boats overland if necessary, in order to make use of the inland lochs and rivers for travel to the innermost regions of Argyll. When Christian missionaries eventually arrived from Ireland during the sixth century, they wisely decided to build their places of worship on the sites chosen by Neolithic man and used for centuries by the native population. In this way the people were encouraged to continue to assemble at the same place, even though the object of their worship had altered.

The church at Dalmally known as Clachan Dysart (saint's retreat), stands on an islet between two branches of the River Orchy and although written evidence of a church on this site dates only from the fourteenth century it is probable that there were earlier Christian buildings. The presence of a pre-Christian hill fort close by suggests that some form of pagan worship may have taken place here also.

St Conan, a contemporary of St Brenden and St Columba, arrived in Argyll from Ireland at some time during the latter half of the sixth century. It is probable that the monk made his way along Loch Awe by currach and landed at the site where Kilchurn Castle now stands. Following the river for a mile or two to the east he came upon a well of good clear water, and having blessed it, built his tiny chapel and set about converting the heathen. St Conan's Well became a place of pilgrimage for many centuries, miracles were associated with it and members of the nobility came in order to benefit from its healing waters. That the village was not only a place of pilgrimage from earliest times but also a place of considerable economic importance is indicated by the presence in the churchyard of the graves of no less than three Scottish kings.

The Rev. Joseph MacIntyre, author of the *Statistical Account* for Glenorchy and Inishail in the 1790s, mentions a man who for many years tended the graveyard and was allowed to live in a bothy beside the well where he conducted visitors to the spot and provided a cup from which they might drink the waters. For this service he would be given a few pence and thereby made his living. When he was about to die the old fellow begged the minister that his house be burned to the ground when he was gone. When the minister entered the building, intending to carry out the old man's wishes, he found the walls had been lined with timber from coffins which had been systematically removed from the kirkyard over the years!

Prior to 1434, most of the land was in the hands of three clans: the MacGregors, the Fletchers and the Campbells. Of these, the MacGregors occupied Glen Strae and were by far the strongest and most powerful group. Their castle and its attendant township was situated at Stronmilchan, a little to the north of Dalmally, and stood on the site of the present Castles Farm. The Castle of Glenstrae, also a MacGregor stronghold, is believed to have stood on the opposite bank of the river from Duiletter, several miles north of Stronmilchan. Not even a ruin remains today of Glenstrae Castle but it is believed to have been a substantial fortress. At the threat of an attack all the occupants of the valley were said to have gathered within the shelter of its walls.

The MacGregors were the first recorded family in Glenstrae. Aodh of Glenorchy, the founder of the clan, called his son Gilla Faolain (devotee of St Fillan). Since St Fillan was the nephew of St Conan, these early references to the MacGregors supposedly allude to a date in the late seventh or early eighth centuries.

In 1040 McGregor Garb (Gregor the Stout) married a Campbell of Lochawe and their son, John of Orchy, married an English lady in the train of Queen Margaret, having two sons by her. The eldest of these was made Baron of Glenstrae and Kilchurn after saving the life of the King (either David or Malcolm III) during a boar hunt. Gregor, the second son, was a great scholar and traveller who became Abbot of Dunkeld and founded the family of MacNab (son of the Abbot), traditional blacksmiths to the MacGregors. Their skill in producing fine weapons and armour was legend throughout Scotland. By 1440 when Kilchurn Castle was under construction, the MacNab blacksmiths were also providing services to the Campbells, becoming heavily involved in the building of the castle.

The MacNabs occupied land at Barachastalain to the south of the present railway station in Dalmally. In the late eighteenth century the French geologist St Fond visited the MacNab household and describes some of the artefacts he saw there, made by the blacksmiths. These included a triclaschodh or three-furrowed steel poniard (dagger) and a wood, leather and brass-studded targe (shield) which had belonged to his host's great-grandfather. The house was described by St Fond as being dug down into the ground for warmth and very dry. It consisted of two rooms and a closet. One room and the closet were filled with stores of oatmeal, barley and peats, neatly stacked ready for the winter. The second room was all but filled by an enormous chimney breast. Inside were wooden stools upon which the members of the household huddled around the peat fire. The only light came from two small windows cut into the chimney itself and, after dark, from a shovel-shaped lamp filled with burning pine-cones. The room was smoky but warm and inviting.

MacNabs continued working as blacksmiths in Dalmally until well into the nineteenth century. One tomb in Dalmally churchyard marks the burying place of a member of the family. Dated 1814, it carries the motto DREAD NOUGHT.

The MacGregors always had a reputation for lawlessness, the most outrageous member of them all being Rob Roy MacGregor. Immortalised by Sir Walter Scott and sanitised by Hollywood, Rob Roy was little more than a robber baron; a cattle thief who terrorised the neighbourhood, collecting protection money even from his own kinsmen. Because he stole the cattle of the rich landowners and distributed his plunder amongst the poor of the parish, he earned for himself the reputation of a latter-day Robin Hood but in the eyes of the authorities he was an outlaw to be hunted down and brought to trial. After ruining the family by losing a fortune in a disastrous cattle deal, he was finally captured and brought to trial. Calling upon the protection of his kinsman, the Duke of Argyll, Rob Roy was spared the gallows but forced to leave Glen Strae for ever. In 1712 he was outlawed, stripped of his lands and property, his wife turned adrift in the snow. The remainder of his life was spent quietly at Balquhidder where he died in 1734.

Glen Orchy was held by the Fletchers, traditionally arrow-makers to the Clan MacGregor. Their stronghold was at Loch Tulla where they built their castle, Achallader, together with the neighbouring township, on the shores of the loch. In 1432 the lands surrounding

Dalmally Churchyard: a MacNab headstone (*Author's Collection*)

Loch Tulla, including Achallader, formed a part of a grant of land made to Sir Colin Campbell by his father, the Duke of Argyll. From then on, although Fletchers still occupied the township beside Loch Tulla, they were resentful tenants of the Campbells. The first mention made of occupation of Achallader by the Campbells themselves was in 1567 when Archibald Campbell received a 'tack of Auchalladour with the keping house thairof'. The original building was replaced *c.* 1600 by Duncan Campbell, 1st Earl of Breadalbane, who had constructed a fortified stone house 'he biggit the toure of Achalladoure, for the workmanship of the quhilk he gaiff ane thousand markis'. In 1603 the house was attacked by Alastair MacGregor of Glenstrae, for which, amongst other crimes, he was executed in 1604. With numerous renovations over the centuries the house remained in occupation at least until the mid-eighteenth century. The present ruins are of a substantial medieval, fortified house, two walls of which are still remaining. Its position on the edge of the wild and lawless Rannoch Moor made Achallader a useful place in which to accommodate the Justice Courts which were held there towards the end of the reign of Charles II in 1683–4 at a period when there was a serious attempt to pacify the Highlands. In 1689 Sir Duncan Campbell objected to proposals that the house be used to garrison the King's troops, it being insufficient to accommodate so large a body of men. Despite Sir Duncan's success in keeping out the army, the house was attacked that same year by elements of the clans Stewart and MacNichol, dissident supporters of the Jacobite cause. Although Duncan had claimed that the house was completely destroyed and had demanded compensation from the Earl of Melville, in fact Achallader was still habitable and remained occupied until the last of the Fletchers moved to Cowal, *c.* 1750.

A little to the west lies the village of Bridge of Orchy, the hotel of which suggests the site of one of the many change-houses set up by order of the Privy Council of James VI. The old drovers used a ford to cross the Orchy but when Major William Caulfield laid his military road through to Glen Coe in the 1750s he built the Bridge of Orchy, which still carries the A82 traffic from the Highlands through to Tyndrum.

The old drovers' road from Glen Coe took the western side of Loch Tulla to the small township of Inveroran. The village boasts an old droving inn which is dated 1708 and appears to have been a substantial if plain three-bay house. It had fallen into some disrepair, however, when in 1804 Dorothy Wordsworth and her brother, William, the poet, made their trip to the Highlands. Travelling from Glencoe to Tyndrum, they came upon the village of Inveroran which Dorothy describes:

> I shall never forget the gentle pleasure with which we greeted the lake of Inveroran and its few grey cottages. Most of the forest had been cut down but there were some single trees left alive as if by their battered black boughs to tell us of the storms that visit the valley . . . when we arrived at the huts, one of them proved to be the inn, a thatched house without a sign board. We were kindly received, had a fire lighted in the parlour but had need of patience before breakfast was brought. About seven or eight drovers with as many dogs were sitting in a complete circle around

Typical rural township, Glenorchy, 1890s (*Easdale Museum*)

a large peat fire in the middle of the floor, each with a mess of porridge, in a wooden vessel, on his knee, a pot suspended from one of the black beams, boiling on the fire, two or three women pursuing their household business and on the outside of the circle, children playing on the floor.

Haldane in his *Drove Roads of Scotland* describes how the drovers relied heavily upon their wise and loyal sheep dogs. He recalls how having arrived at the trysts at Dumbarton or Falkirk and having disposed of their charges, the drovers might continue on south to the border country where there was work to be had in the harvesting or ploughing. A drover would thereupon order his dog to make his own way home. The animal would retrace their route calling at the various stances along the way to rest and be fed by the landlord. On returning himself, later in the year, the drover would repay the innkeepers for their care of the dog!

The Inveroran Hotel was refurbished and extended in 1855. During the first half of the nineteenth century, the Earl of Breadalbane decided to build a hunting lodge (Forest Lodge) a mile or two from

Inveroran. Fearing the noise and smells of the passing sheep and cattle, he had the drovers' road diverted around the other side of the loch. His plan included moving the stance to the new road and closer to Tyndrum. The drovers, incensed at Breadalbane's high-handed decision, took the matter to the courts where they were judged to have inalienable rights to continue to use Inveroran as their resting place. Breadalbane lost his case and the stance remained at Inveroran until the first decade of the twentieth century.

The Campbells occupied the lands surrounding the eastern end of Loch Awe and the valley of the River Lochy as well as large areas of Argyll in Lorne and south towards Campbeltown. In 1445 Sir Duncan Campbell was created Lord of Lochow while his successor became the 1st Earl of Argyll. From Sir Duncan's younger son, Colin Campbell of Glenorchy, descended the Earls and Marquises of Breadalbane.

In 1308, as a reward for supporting Robert the Bruce against the MacDougalls of Lorn, Sir Neil Campbell was given the land round the head of Loch Awe. Taking advantage of the exile of the chief of the MacGregors, who had been captured by Edward I and sent away to France, Sir Neil Campbell married his second son John, to MacGregor's infant daughter, Mariota, thereby securing the lands of Glenstrae. In 1357 John Campbell received a formal charter for his wife's lands from King David II. The Campbells were now free to occupy the ancient stronghold of the MacGregors, Kilchurn Castle, at the head of Loch Awe. In 1440, the Superiority of Glenorchy passed to Colin Campbell, the brother of the future Duke of Argyll. Glenstrae, however, remained in the Superiority of the Duke himself and the MacGregors were retained as his tenants.

Colin Campbell was a remarkable character. He travelled three times to Rome, was created Knight of Rhodes and became the founder of the House of Breadalbane. Having begun the rebuilding of Kilchurn castle, he left the work in the hands of his wife while he went on a crusade to Spain to fight against the Moor invasion. Mariot, or Margaret, engaged the blacksmith MacNab to help with the rebuilding of the castle. By the time her husband returned seven years later, the work was nearly completed.

The fifteenth-century castle of Kilchurn appears to rise out of the waters at the head of Loch Awe but is, in fact, built on a rocky promontory which is cut off on the landward side by a bog and may well have been an island at one time. The castle was only

Kilchurn Castle, by P. Hazell – lithograph (*Author's Collection*)

spasmodically occupied by the Glenorchy Campbells although various other members of the clan served as its Steward.

The original structure was a plain tower house but before the beginning of the sixteenth century a laich hall was added to the south-west wall of the castle. At the end of the seventeenth century a four-storey barracks block was created to the north-west side and angle towers were added to the curtain walls. Although garrisoned throughout the Jacobite disturbances, Kilchurn was abandoned soon after and the roof of Easdale slates was removed to be reused in the reconstruction of Inveraray Castle. The building was consolidated in the 1960s by the Department of the Environment (Ancient Monuments Division). Recently there have been proposals to rebuild part of the structure and to convert the castle to a hotel.

Colin Campbell outlived Mariot and three other wives, dying at the age of eighty. As reward for helping the King (James III) in the arrest of Thomas Chambers, one of the murderers of James I of Scotland, he was given Chambers' lands of Lawers on Loch Tay. It was here at Taymouth that the Breadalbane branch of the family eventually built a permanent home which they occupied until the beginning of the twentieth century.

In 1625 Sir Duncan Campbell, having, so it is said, supplied King James VI and I with a gift of a capercaillie for his park at Windsor, was made Baronet of Nova Scotia!

Despite his reputation for avariciousness and cruelty Sir Duncan made many improvements in the parish. As well as restoring Kilchurn Castle, he planted forests in Glenorchy leaving a rich heritage of timber to his successors. He rebuilt the church at Dalmally and, it is thought, provided for a minister in the parish and contributed to the cost of constructing the Dalmally bridge which crosses the River Orchy at Stronmilchan. This three-arched bridge and its accompanying causeway, which give access to the Dalmally parish church of Clachan Dysart, was constructed to a plan similar to that of the Bridge of Awe, destroyed in a flash flood in the 1990s.

Perhaps Breadalbane's greatest contribution to the parish was in introducing new farming methods. Having studied farming in many countries of Europe he brought order to the system applied in Glenorchy, determining what crops should be grown and regularising the use of common pastures for the benefit of all the farmers. Until the end of the eighteenth century, goats and small black cattle were the mainstay of agriculture in the valleys. Digging was accomplished by use of the cas chrom, a hand-operated plough. Barley for making bread was grown on the better land but bere, a variety of barley growing well on poor soil, was considered the best for whisky distilling which then, as now, was strictly controlled. In 1627 a case was brought before Sir Duncan Campbell's Court 'to hiding the distiller and to drinking a boddach' (a measure of whisky: about a pint).

Oats were always a main crop but by the seventeenth century potatoes had been introduced. Apart from their use as a staple of the diet, these provided starch for laundry and formed the basis of a potent alcoholic beverage. When times were particularly hard the potato was also mixed with other ingredients to make a kind of bread jelly and a very poor substitute for cheese. There were a number of mills in the glen, one of which remains today as a saw mill standing beside a bridge over the River Lochy.

In his *Statistical Account* of the parish written in the years 1791–9, Rev. Joseph MacIntyre condemned the import of 1,000 bolls of grain per annum into a district which should be able to fulfil all the culinary needs of its inhabitants from its own cultivation. He attributed these excessive imports to the unwholesome habit of growing bere instead of oats and of distilling whisky. He was ashamed to have to record that the village shop in Dalmally sold £60 worth of snuff and tobacco each year, condemning the parishioners for a wanton use of their meagre resources: 'Let the men however continue to do as they chose [sic] but far be it for the fair and respectable females of this vale to disfigure their features and destroy their powers of song and sweet cadence by a habit so repugnant of everything engaging and cleanly in women.' MacKintyre regarded whisky as 'a deleterious spirit ruinous to health and industry and to morals. If no spirit were distilled in the county the quantity of meal to be imported would be a trifle.'

The Rev. MacIntyre made no mention of the hordes of drovers passing through the village in great numbers at certain periods of every year. Surely they must have been the greatest consumers of both tobacco and whisky and there is little doubt that his parishioners made a great deal more money from these sales than from baking bread.

In the main the Campbells supported the Reformation and were staunchly Presbyterian. Although they made enemies of the MacDougalls of Lorne as well as the MacGregors and the Fletchers, and generally receive a bad press from that quarter, down the centuries the Breadalbane Campbells, like the Dukes of Argyll, put much of their extraordinary wealth back into the land, exploiting the county's material assets and its agricultural land while at the same time encouraging the talents and improving the condition of the ordinary people. The Breadalbanes provided good housing for their tenants, churches and schools. They subscribed to building roads and bridges and, in the nineteenth century, supported the efforts of the Callander & Oban Railway Company to open up the remote Highlands.

While the first villages in the parish were almost certainly those townships lying outwith the walls of the clan strongholds, later settlement depended more upon economic factors such as resources and communications than upon tribal loyalties. Dalmally became the natural centre of the parish and Clachan Dysart its parish church.

There are many explanations for the village's success as a settlement. Lying as it does, ten miles east of the village of Taynuilt, Dalmally was the obvious choice for a drovers' stance. It stands at the meeting of two main roads and at the head of a massive inland waterway and was visited frequently by the most influential of travellers through the Highlands.

Glenorchy Church, Dalmally (*Author's Collection*)

The original Dalmally drovers' inn was built on the site of the present cattle market but in the mid-eighteenth century Lewis Pickard built a three-bay, three-storey building on the present site which was extended by the addition of a west wing in 1841–4. Thomas Pennant in his account of his journey through the Highlands in 1769 speaks of staying at a good inn where after breakfast he was 'present at a christening and became sponsor to a little Highlander by no other ceremony than receiving him for a moment in my arms: this is a mere act of friendship and no essential rite in the church of Scotland'. Dorothy and William Wordsworth visited the Dalmally Inn in 1804.

The church at Dalmally has been the parish church from earliest recorded history. Mention is made of Fintan Mundus who on his death in 635 was described as Abbot of Kilmund and Dissert, but other than St Conan who died in 648, the next priest mentioned is Maelog who had a retreat or dyseart here – hence the name Clachan Dysart. In 1449 a Charter was witnessed by Sir Gavin, the Curate of Dysart, and in 1498, 1510 and 1523 Gilbert Boorach is described as the vicar of Dysart. There is an excellent record of the ministers who followed which is available in the church. Of particular note is one John McVean MA, whose stone stands in the churchyard. Apart from his duties as minister between 1736 and 1764 he was also valued in the district for his knowledge of surgery.

Over the centuries many references have been made to the condition of the buildings on this site. One imagines endless temporary repairs being carried out, none of them particularly satisfactory. In 1615 a medieval church (1440) was rebuilt by Sir Duncan Campbell of Glenorchy. Campbell gave 'ane thousand pundis monie for the building and reparinge of the kirk of Glenurqhuay callit Clachandysert being altogidder rowinus and decayit'. By 1807 this building was declared unsafe. The 4th Earl of Breadalbane was responsible for raising the money to rebuild Dalmally Church in 1809 and for engaging the Edinburgh architect James Elliot, brother of the better-known Archibald. His design included the unusual octagonal nave which gives the building such a distinctive appearance. The square tower with the main entrance at its base, rises to a height of 25.5 m. The bell was a gift of the parishioners in 1883 and the clock, whose mechanism is contained within the tower, was the gift of the Marchioness of Breadalbane in 1914.

Timber for the roof was provided from Breadalbane's forests in Glenstrae. Stone from his own quarries and slate from Easdale reduced the cost of building which was estimated at 800 guineas in 1810. Further repairs were made to the church in 1898 at which time the stained-glass window was added. Again in 1930 repairs and extensions followed the union of the Dalmally Church with the Free Church of Scotland, at which time the Free Church building became the church hall.

Of the graveyard at Dalmally Thomas Pennant wrote in 1769:

> In the churchyard are several grave stones of great antiquity, with figures of a warrior, each furnished with a spear or two-handed sword; on some are representations of the chase; on others elegant fretwork; and on one, said to be part of the coffin of a McGregor, is a fine running pattern of foliage and flowers and excepting the figures, all in good taste.

Glenorchy Church, Dalmally – mort-safe (*Author's Collection*)

Sadly most of these stones are now heavily encrusted with moss and lichen and the decoration defaced by time. In 1820 Robert Southey who built the present church, wrote 'a great proportion of the grave stones bear the name of Campbell'. In fact, the Campbell graves are in a separate enclosure protected by a wall some two metres in height. Southey objected to the Scottish habit of engraving 'skulls and other such hideous emblems of mortality'. Of MacNab's stone he says 'here upon a smith's his pincers hammer and bellows were sculptured'. One remarkable feature is an early nineteenth-century mort-safe which could be placed over a new grave to protect it from grave robbers.

A poignant reminder of the tinkers, that itinerant workforce once so important to agriculture throughout the Highlands, is a grassy corner formed by the incurving of the churchyard wall. Here one family of tinkers who passed regularly through the village buried their children. Each spring the family left small baskets of flowers on the graves and at other times the village children tended the spot.

In the early 1900s Breadalbane, quick to take advantage of the demands of newly rich barons of industry seeking to acquire estates in the Highlands, began to sell off parcels of land in Glenorchy. To do this he was obliged to move many of his cottars off the hill pastures and fertile lower slopes, offering them new houses and plots of land on the alluvial plain on either side of the river. While some took up his offer, others quit the valley altogether. The new leaseholders built their mansions and hunting lodges, stocked their rivers with game fish and cleared the sheep and cattle from the hillside, erecting fences where once people and animals had roamed freely. Without the intensive grazing of former times, the land was quickly covered by heath and bracken and was of little use for anything other than providing cover for the grouse.

With such a long ecclesiastical history the parish must have had schools for a long time. In the 1791 *Statistical Account* the Rev. MacIntyre remarks upon the literacy of most of the parishioners. The Dalmally School originally stood beside the limekiln at Auchtermally, south of the railway station and close to the MacNab's property. The children came to it, each carrying a peat for the fire, but only after the milking had been done and wool carded ready for their parents to spin. According to MacIntyre, in the 1790s the school at Dalmally had a good reputation and besides the local children it had pupils from the West Indies. At that time there was a substantial trade in roofing slates between Easdale and the British West Indies, which may account for the presence of these little visitors from abroad. The schoolmaster's salary was £40, £15 of which was supplied by Breadalbane and the remainder from various sources within the parish including a small fee paid by the children themselves. The number of pupils on role depended upon the season. In winter as many as one hundred pupils attended. In the spring and summer months the numbers dwindled as work intensified on the farms. At harvest the schoolmaster declared a holiday, the length of which depended upon the size of the harvest and the nature of the weather.

The parish of Glenorchy and Inishail boasts at least one famous Gaelic poet, Duncan Ban MacIntyre, who died in 1812 at the age of eighty-eight. His memorial, a circular peristyle of Appin stone stands on Dunach Hill where the old military road climbs south-west from Dalmally.

The part of the parish to the south side of Loch Awe was once a separate parish which included the island of Inishail and the villages of Portsonachan and Cladich. The only building on the island of Inishail which lies in Loch Awe opposite the outfall of the River Awe is a ruined chapel, at one time the parish church of Inishail. The earliest recorded date for an ecclesiastical building on the site is 1257.

Portsonachan was an important drovers' stance receiving herds of cattle ferried across the loch from Kilchrennan and Dalavich. Today the village comprises a group of houses and a hotel and holiday complex which are confined to a narrow strip of flatter ground between the loch shore and the Aray forest.

The village of Cladich originally lay alongside the main road from Inveraray. Dorothy Wordsworth records her stay at the inn in rather uncomplimentary terms, but describes the delight with which she first spied Loch Awe from the summit of the hill. The village, now bypassed, consists of no more than a small group of cottages with neither inn nor school.

Ten miles to the east of Dalmally, on the border of Argyll with Stirlingshire, lies the village of Tyndrum. Despite a number of politically motivated changes to county or regional boundaries which have left Tyndrum sometimes in and sometimes out of Argyll, this busy little settlement has traditionally been included within the parish of Glenorchy and Inishail.

Tyndrum stands at the junction of roads, one to Glen Coe and Fort William in the north-west and another due west to Oban. Situated at the head of two major valleys it is the source of two rivers, to the east the River Fillan and to the west the River Lochy. Its unique position determined the importance of the spot from earliest times. With its strath of lush pasture Tyndrum became a natural site for a drovers' stance and on the spot were established a hostelry, a few crofts providing food for the drovers as well as the local inhabitants and such essential facilities as a bootmaker and a blacksmith. Throughout the centuries the settlement has survived as little more than a row of dwellings straddling the main road, its economy dependent upon passing trade.

At least two attempts have been made to develop an industry in Tyndrum, at 250 m above sea level the most elevated village in Argyll. Lead was discovered in the 1830s and was mined until well into the nineteenth century. In his *First Tour of Scotland 1769*, Thomas Pennant reports: 'A lead mine is worked here by a level to some advantage; was discovered about thirty years ago; the veins run SW and NE.' The mine, which was successfully worked by the London Lead Company, was leased from the Earl of Breadalbane in exchange for 6 per cent of the value of lead bars from smelting.

Because a small quantity of silver was obtained during the process

Typical lead workings of the eighteenth century (*Author's Collection*)

of lead extraction the mine at Tyndrum was declared Royal. The silver, three halfpennies from every one pound of lead, belonged to the Crown. In more recent times gold too has been found in the same seams. Experiments have been carried out since the mid twentieth century to exploit the deposits but so far extraction has proved to be uneconomical

The second and more substantial enterprise concerns the work of the Forestry Commission which planted thousands of acres of conifers during the 1930s and subsequently. To accommodate the influx of workers for this project the Commission built a row of cottages in the centre of the village, thereby doubling the housing stock at that time. Although forestry still plays an important role in the economy of the district, the Commission houses are now privately owned and the number of those employed in the industry has been substantially reduced. The late twentieth century attempt to improve the appearance of the afforested areas by increasing the acreage planted with hardwoods has paid off handsomely in terms of the tourism industry. The overall appearance of the environment has been significantly improved and in the autumn special tours are offered to view the autumn colours.

Today Tyndrum is a popular watering place for travellers to the west coast. The oldest hotel, built on the site of the original drovers'

Autumn at Loch Awe (*Author's Collection*)

stance has been joined by substantial new developments. The village has become a centre for climbers and walkers as well as gold prospectors. Employment today is concentrated almost entirely upon the hospitality industry.

Tyndrum is the gateway into Argyll on its eastern border and the exit route for visitors who are homeward bound. In every way the village fulfils its purpose, providing information, sustenance and shelter for travellers in much the same way as it did when there was nothing here but a drovers' change-house and the passing traffic moved on four feet. It is a far cry from the days when Queen Victoria took this road in the Earl of Breadalbane's wagonette and Dorothy and William Wordsworth passed through in their one horse-powered 'car'.

In 2004, the car parks with space for a few hundred cars and coaches bear witness to the huge numbers of travellers passing this point every day. It is a measure of the vastness of the open spaces of Argyll that once the crowds cross the county boundary, they seem to be swallowed up within the landscape. With careful management there is no reason why the tourism industry should do anything but enhance the peace and solitude, the tranquillity of mind and spirit which this beautiful county offers to those who choose to come here.

ACKNOWLEDGEMENTS

The book has been informed by the following:

HMSO Royal Commission on the Ancient and Historical Monuments of Scotland. Argyll Vols I and VII, 1975 et seq.

West Highland Steamers by Duckworth and Langmuir, 1967, T. Stevenson and Sons

The Callander and Oban Railway by John Thomas, 1966, David St. John Thomas

Victorian Travel on the West Highland Morr and Loch by Sir Joseph Causton and Son, 1896, republished by House of Lochar 2002

Ferry Tales of Argyll and the Isles by Walter Weyndling, 1996, Alan Sutton

Clyde Pleasure Steamers by Ian MacCrorie, 1987, Orr, Pollock and Co.

A Journey through England and Scotland by B. Faujas de St Fond, 1784

A Tour of Scotland by Thomas Pennant, 1769, reprint by Birlinn, 2000

Tour of Scotland by Dorothy Wordsworth, 1803, reprint by Mercat Press, 1974

Netherlorn and its Neighbourhood by Patrick H. Gillies, 1909, Virtue

Inveraray and the Dukes of Argyll by Ian G. Lindsay and Mary Cosh, 1973, EUP

Queen Victoria's Highland Journeys ed. by David Duff, 1980, Webb & Bower

A Description of the Western Isles written by Martin Martin, ed. by D. MacLeod, 1994, Birlinn

Reminiscences of Scottish Life and Character by Dean Ramsay, c.1872, T.N. Foulis

Highland Folk Ways by J.F.Grant, 1975, Routledge

Drove Roads of Scotland by A.R.B. Haldane, 1997, Birlinn

Return to Loch Fyne written and privately published by Eoin McArthur, 2003

Historic Argyll (various vols.), Lorn Archeological and Historical Society Publications

Night Falls on Ardnamurchan by Alasdair Maclean, 2001, Birlinn

An Official Short History of the Clan Mac Dougall written and privately published by Michael Starforth

Walking Around Oban, Walking in North Lorn, Walking in South Lorn, Exploring Sunart, Ardnamurchan, Moidart and Morar, West Highland Series, Harlequin Press, Oban

Inveraray Tales and Traditions written and privately published by Donald MacKechnie

Taynuilt Our History compiled by T.H.L. MacDonald, 1966, Taynuilt Public Hall Management Committee

Appin and District Visitor Guide, c. 2000, Appin Historical Society

Lead and Lead Mining by Lynn Willies, 1999, Shire

The Slate Industry by Merfyn Williams, 2002, Shire

The Islands that Roofed the World by Mary Withall, 2000, Luath Press

Archives of Argyll and Bute Council, Lochgilphead
Archives of Easdale Museum, Easdale
Archives of Slate Islands Heritage Trust, Ellenabeich, Isle of Seil
National Archives of Scotland, Scottish Records Office, Edinburgh
Statistical Accounts of Argyll 1791 to 1961

My thanks are due to the staff of the Scottish Records Office, Edinburgh; to Murdo McDonald, Archivist for Argyll and Bute; staff of the Oban library; the Kilmartin Museum Librarian; Michael Shaw for permission to use the Kilbrandon House Library; Jean Adams, Curator Easdale Museum and Director of the Scottish Slate Islands Heritage Trust; Charles Hunter and members of the Lorn Archaeological and Historical Society; to various church historians whose explanatory pamphlets provided the basis for further research and members of the Scottish Rural Women's Institute, whose entries to a competition organised by the central office of the institute, provided a wealth of detail of village life in Argyll. In particular I would like to thank members of the Taynuilt branch whose fascinating entry (Taynuilt – Our Village) was chosen from 13 parishes to represent Argyll in the competition. My thanks are due also to my colleague Marian Pallister (author of *The Villages of Southern Argyll*) for suggestions and encouragement and to my husband Peter for taking new and processing old photographs, driving endless miles and consuming many a pint in pursuit of local colour!